FOCUSED & FEARLESS LEADERSHIP

Praise for "Focused and Fearless Leadership: Preventing the Crisis Before It Starts"

"Great leaders are powerful storytellers. You can search the Internet for information. You can ask AI for advice or direction. But stories are more valuable than lists and bullet points and disjointed facts.

I love Melissa's book, 'Focused & Fearless Leadership', because it teaches leadership through fascinating stories that illustrate important principles. She doesn't just tell you. She shows you by bringing you into the intense and extraordinary experiences she's had throughout her life and career."

— David Rendall, author of *The Freak Factor, The Freak Factor for Kids, Pink Goldfish,* and *The Four Factors of Effective Leadership,* international Certified Speaking Professional, and Ironman athlete

"This book is a trusted companion for anyone seeking to grow with purpose, laugh with intention, and lead with heart. My favorite is "lead with heart"; I wish I could claim those as my words."

— Suzanne Ross, business expert, North Central Regional Director, NC Small Business Center

"Melissa's brilliance is that she puts the work on both sides: knowing your style is easy; flexing it is where leadership begins. Instead of dismissing spontaneous ideas or letting them derail the plan, she teaches us to build a tiny on-ramp, one that preserves their energy without short-circuiting my system.

Practical, funny, and immediately useful."

— Kristina Hanny, PMP - business leader and Certified Sr Project Manager

"More than a leadership manual, this is an authentic, timely, and practical guide to what high-performance leadership truly looks and feels like, a must-read for seasoned professionals and emerging leaders alike."

— Heidi Marie Stieber, business leader & world traveler, President and Founder: HMS Insights Consulting

"There are people who know leadership, and there are people who live it. Melissa is one of the few who does both. Credibility isn't built by what we say. It's built by the life we live. I trust this book because I've watched Melissa lead long before she wrote it.

If you're serious about becoming a better leader, learn from people whose lives have earned the right to teach. Melissa has earned that right. This is the kind of book every leader should own, every team should discuss, and every organization would benefit from placing in the hands of its people."

— Cornelius Kirk, Founder The Family Code and The Bold Stand

"Throughout my career in real estate and my service as President of the Clayton Rotary Club, I've learned that great leadership starts with intentionality.'Focused & Fearless Leadership' delivers practical, actionable strategies for leading with clarity, strength-ening relationships, and staying focused on what matters most.

The insights are relevant, impactful, and immediately applicable. I highly recommend this book to anyone looking to grow as a leader in business or their community".

— Lynn Roman, professional Broker/REALTOR®, Rotary Club President (past)

"Captivating, relatable, and refreshingly real, 'Focused & Fearless Leadership' turns everyday moments into powerful leadership lessons. Melissa's storytelling draws you in, while her reflection questions challenge you to look inward and put those lessons into action. As one 'orange' to another (if you know, you know) - I felt her authenticity, energy, and heart on every page. Whatever your personality or leadership experience, this book will speak to you, stretch you, and leave you better equipped to lead."

—Dana Wooten, IOM award-winning Chamber executive, President & CEO at The Clayton Chamber of Commerce

FOCUSED & FEARLESS LEADERSHIP

Preventing the Crisis
Before It Starts

MELISSA GODWIN OVERTON

THE OVERTON EXPERIENCE

Cover & Graphics by: Heidi Marie Stieber
Editing by: Ann Buskirk & Heidi Marie Stieber
Published by: The Overton Experience
Book formatting by: Carlene_Edits & WordXense | Saqib Arshad

ISBN: 979-8-9952771-0-1

FOCUSED /ˈfō-kəst/

1: Directing attention, energy, and decisions with clarity toward what matters most.

2: Maintaining disciplined alignment between priorities, actions, and outcomes, especially under pressure.

3: The ability to filter noise, eliminate distraction, and act with intentional precision.

FEARLESS /ˈfeer-ləs/

1: Acting with courage and conviction despite uncertainty, risk, or discomfort.

2: Willing to address hard truths, make decisive choices, and lead through tension without avoidance.

3: Not the absence of fear, but the mastery of it in service of purpose and progress.

For every leader who was handed
responsibility without a roadmap,
who was told to "figure it out"
without training, tools, or a title.

This book is for you.

You are *not* alone, and you are much
more capable than you know.

At KS Bank, we believe leadership is more than a title, it's a calling, especially in times of crisis.

I've had the privilege of working closely with Melissa Overton as she coached and trained our management teams and employees. She brings not only an extraordinary depth of experience as a nurse and emergency responder but also a rare ability to translate real-life intensity into practical, empowering leadership lessons.

Melissa's approach is personal, grounded, and refreshingly honest. *Focused and Fearless Leadership* doesn't just offer theory; it's built from the front lines of trauma rooms, boardrooms, and everyday life. Her background as a Registered Nurse, Entrepreneur, Community Leader and Certified John Maxwell Trainer, Speaker and Coach gives her unique insight into human behavior, communication, and crisis leadership. But what makes this book truly special is Melissa herself - her resilience, her humor, and her unwavering belief in people.

This is more than a book. It's a guide for anyone who wants to lead well when things go wrong- and an invitation to lead better every day.

Melissa has impacted our organization, and I have no doubt she'll impact you, too.

— Earl W. Worley, Jr.
President & CEO, KS Bank

As a new graduate nurse in the late 1990s, I was working night shift in a small community emergency department. It was a typical evening; the steady rhythm of true emergencies mixed with complaints that could have waited until morning.

The only available room that night was the OB/GYN room, equipped with a table, stirrups, and a couple of chairs. A psychiatric patient had just arrived and was placed there for privacy, which felt preferable to leaving him in the waiting room. He was accompanied by his elderly mother and a local law enforcement officer.

The officer's presence meant the situation was serious. A judge had issued a mandate requiring the patient to receive medical evaluation despite his refusal. He posed a risk to himself or others.

The patient stood about six foot five and weighed easily three hundred fifty pounds. He had schizophrenia and had stopped taking his medication again. His exhausted mother sat quietly in the corner, heartbroken and praying, while her son's brief moments of calm were interrupted by aggressive arm swings and rapid, uneven breathing.

The officer assigned to watch him was young and visibly annoyed. During one docile moment, he removed the patient's handcuffs. As the patient's agitation escalated again, several staff members pulled the officer aside and urged him to put them back on.

He refused.

He vented his frustration about being stuck "babysitting" in the ER while his colleagues were out doing "real" police work in the community.

I moved in and out of the area as I cared for my other patients that night. In the room next door, I was preparing to start an IV on an overly emotional man who was deeply concerned about being stuck with a needle. I approached him with kindness and a little ribbing, using humor to break the tension and distract him from the unpleasantness.

Suddenly, a blood-curdling scream erupted from the room next door. There was banging. Feet shuffled violently across the floor.

It had happened.

I released the tourniquet from my patient's arm and ran toward the noise.

From the doorway, I took in the scene in a split second. The patient's mother was pressed into a corner near the sink, frozen in fear. On the opposite side of the room, the patient had the officer pinned against the wall. He narrowly missed a metal hook holding sterilized speculum packages. Had he hit it, the officer would have been impaled and killed instantly.

The screaming was deafening. My ears rang as I tried to process what I was seeing and decide how to respond.

The officer's hands were shielding his head and face, leaving his firearm exposed as the patient pummeled him repeatedly. The officer was maybe five foot eight and weighed no more than one hundred fifty pounds. It was a losing battle.

I stepped one foot into the room and immediately stepped back out, my commonsense kicking in just in time. If I stood up very straight, I was five foot three.

What in the world was I going to do?

I scanned the department for help. Our security guards had not arrived yet, and even when they did, they were elderly men who would be seriously injured if they tried to intervene. The unit secretary, Miss Gladora, was already walking away, repeating "Uh-uh" under her breath as she retreated to safety. The nurse who had trained me, a woman who never panicked about anything, was frantically dialing 911.

This was the highest level of chaos I had experienced in my professional life.

Everyone was in danger.

The only other man working that night was Billy. God bless Billy. He was a nursing assistant and a Vietnam veteran, standing about six foot two. I screamed his name at the top of my lungs.

He looked up, instantly understood, and took off running.

Billy crossed the nurses' station and launched himself into the room. Like a puma, he lunged onto the patient's back, wrapping his arm around the patient's neck and pulling him off the officer in a choke hold. The patient stopped hitting the officer and began flailing violently, trying to throw Billy off.

Billy's glasses shattered. His face was cut.

At the same time, the phone was ringing nonstop. The secretary was still hiding, so I grabbed it. It was the 911 communications center.

Thank God.

The operator asked if we truly had an emergency. I said, "Yes. Please tell me help is coming."

She replied that officers were at the ambulance bay trying to get in. The hospital had installed a new code lock on the doors just the week before and the police and 911 were not aware of the code.

I ran to the door and motioned to activate it. Four or five officers rushed in and helped Billy force the patient to the floor, directly in front of the man who had been so emotional about getting an IV.

As officers restrained the patient, I lunged forward and put my full weight onto the back of his thigh. Another staff member rushed in with sedation medication and handed it to me. I administered it quickly and stayed in position with the officers, holding him down until the medication took effect.

It felt like seconds and an eternity all at once.

Eventually, the patient went limp. The fight was over.

I lifted my head and took in the department. When chaos erupts, I tend to narrow my focus to only what must be done. Now, awareness rushed back in.

Billy and the officer were being treated by staff. The police officers were communicating over their radios. The sedated patient was transferred to a bed and reassessed for ongoing care.

I stood up, brushed myself off, and washed my hands.

Then I walked back into the room with the man who still needed an IV.

He was silent. Shocked. The entire takedown had happened right in front of him.

I tucked my hair behind my ears, pushed up my sleeves, and smiled. "Are you still going to whine about getting this IV?" I asked, winking.

He laughed nervously and held out his arm without another word. After that, I started the IV and then had a hell of a lot of paperwork to do.

There are a few reasons I share this story with you.

1. I have always been fascinated by how people respond in a crisis. At this point in my career, there had been no formal training or protocols for managing violent or aggressive patients. We were all winging it, relying on instinct, adrenaline, and whatever courage we could muster in the moment.

2. In 20+ years of critical care and leadership experience, I have learned that most emergencies don't come out of nowhere. They escalate because we ignore the early signs. In this situation, a lack of collaboration between ER staff and law enforcement (and the officer's refusal to reapply the handcuffs) were early indicators.

Knowing what I know now, I would have requested medication early to prevent escalation. Emergencies grow in the gaps: the things we don't say, don't request, don't question, or don't prepare for.

3. In healthcare, you learn quickly how to compartmentalize. There was no debrief, no time-out, no emotional processing. Just paperwork, tasks, and moving on to the next crisis. This is true in leadership too. Many of us are never taught how to reflect, recover, or learn from the emergencies we survive.

This moment was also my first glimpse into what I now call *Focused and Fearless Leadership*.

Focused leaders pay attention to patterns, people, and the early warning signs that something is shifting. They see what's really happening beneath the surface, whether in a patient, a project, a team dynamic, or a culture.

Fearless leaders act on what they see. They speak up, intervene, redirect, question, clarify, and prepare before the moment turns into a full-blown emergency.

In the ER, in that moment, none of us had those words yet, but the absence of Focused and Fearless Leadership was obvious. And once you know what to look for, you'll see it everywhere: In boardrooms, in teams, in communities, in families, *and* in your own life.

Leadership emergencies rarely come from the crisis itself. They come from what we missed (and what we ignored) before it happened.

This book is about learning to see those moments sooner and respond to them with clarity, courage, and confidence. It is about leading in a way that prevents the crisis before it starts.

Welcome to **Focused and Fearless Leadership**.

CHAPTER 01

Leadership Emergencies Occur Throughout Life

"Focused leaders reflect on life lessons. Fearless leaders build on them."

We were four years old when my stepbrother found a lighter and wanted to use it inside our home. I can still see myself standing there with my cousin, trying to negotiate a better choice, as if a preschooler could reason with another child holding fire.

By the time I was eight, I was running peace talks between two adults who were supposed to be raising me.

These were the first moments that forced me into what I now call Focused and Fearless Leadership. I had to focus to survive, and I had to be fearless long before I had language for what I was doing.

A leadership moment is not defined by a title or a job. It is any moment when the absence of healthy leadership turns a difficult situation into a dangerous one. These moments show up when emotions run high, clarity is missing, and the next decision can make things better or much worse.

They do not begin in boardrooms. They begin in living rooms, kitchens, behind closed doors, and in the quiet places where we learn how to survive before we ever learn how to lead.

I was driven and a natural connector even as a child. Leadership came easily to me as the oldest sibling. On days when home felt safe, or when the weather allowed us to escape it, I organized dance contests, singing competitions, and Sunday afternoon softball games. What did not come naturally was having leaders in my home.

My upbringing was anything but traditional. I like to say I earned a bird's-eye view of communication styles, conflict strategies, and emotional instability long before I could define any of it.

My biological father lived with undiagnosed bipolar disorder. One moment he was defeated, the next energized by a business idea that promised to "make us rich." Alcohol often intensified both his highs and his lows. My stepmother carried her own unaddressed struggles, and together they created a home that could shift from calm to chaos without warning.

Between the ages of eight and thirteen, I became the household mediator. I pulled each parent aside during threats to leave and tried to help them see the other's perspective. I was being abused by both of them in different ways, yet somehow being with them together felt safer than being alone with either one. I tried to hold our family together not out of naivety, but out of survival for myself, my stepbrother, and my little sister.

"Craziness," as I understood it then, looked like laundry washed but never folded, piled into a mountain you had to dig through to find something to wear. It looked like fish sticks and homemade biscuits, the only things I knew how to cook when no one else would. It looked like moments when my stepmother was high, ironically the only times she seemed able to tolerate me. It looked like tucking my sheets tightly under me at night so I might wake up before someone's hands found me in the dark.

I stayed quiet because telling the truth threatened whatever fragile stability we had. At thirteen, I finally spoke up. Not because I was fearless, but because I was terrified of losing the last piece of innocence I had left.

That disclosure became its own crisis, but it was also the doorway out.

My aunt, who many people in my life know as my "mom," took me in. She gave me safety, structure, and permission to simply be Melissa.

Those experiences shaped me long before I understood how. They taught me to read a room quickly, anticipate danger, de-escalate conflict, and communicate clearly when everything around me was falling apart. I did not call it leadership. I called it survival.

But survival skills often become leadership foundations.

Life rarely gives us the leadership curriculum we want, but it always gives us the lessons we need. Those early experiences became the first bricks in the framework I now teach. The moments that nearly break us often shape us the most. They sharpen our clarity, deepen our compassion, and strengthen our courage.

Focused leaders reflect on life.
Fearless leaders build on it.

By high school, I gravitated toward psychology and medicine, my first conscious attempts to understand people, pain, and healing. When psychology did not feel like the right fit and becoming a physician felt too confining, nursing appeared almost by accident.

It felt like the perfect intersection of what fascinated me most: the mind and the body, illness and healing, compassion and crisis.

What I did not yet know was that nursing, particularly emergency medicine, would become the ultimate training ground for Focused and Fearless Leadership.

In the emergency department, crises do not wait for permission. They arrive unannounced, unravel quickly, and demand immediate clarity. Long before I understood clinical protocols or leadership theory, I learned this truth as a teenager volunteering in the ER. I was not supposed to get hands-on at seventeen, but when people needed help, rules became secondary. I remember palpating a ruptured Achilles tendon after a man went down during a neighborhood basketball game. Another day, I stood frozen, staring at a severed finger sitting in a cup of ice, until a nurse joked that she wanted it sewn to her forehead so she could point people in the right direction.

That twisted sense of humor was not accidental. It was survival. And strangely, I loved it.

What hooked me was not just the adrenaline. It was the way crisis revealed people. When others froze or fled, I leaned in. My instinct was to focus on the next solvable problem. Chaos brought clarity. Even then, I was fascinated by how differently people responded under pressure. Some escalated. Some created calm. Some communicated clearly. Others made everything worse.

I did not know it at the time, but I was already cataloging patterns that would later shape how I teach leaders.

While in nursing school, I immersed myself fully. I worked in a university emergency department as both a nursing assistant and unit secretary so I could absorb everything: clinical care, communication, systems, and flow. I also joined a volunteer paramedic EMS unit because a nurse I deeply admired worked there. Donna was one of the smartest people I had ever met and one of the first Sexual Assault Nurse Examiners in North Carolina. She was a pioneer, brilliant and unflappable. Watching her confirmed something for me.

Credibility in crisis does not come from bravado. It comes from competence, calm, and clarity.

After graduation, I was hired as an ER nurse at a small community hospital. During my interview, I was blunt, probably too blunt. I told my manager, Suzie, that I might only stay a year and that I did not want to become a jaded nurse who stopped learning. In hindsight, I would never have hired me. I was ambitious, opinionated, and convinced I was destined for bigger organizations.

Suzie saw something beyond my boldness and lack of filter. She hired me anyway.

Suzie became my first true leadership mirror. She gave me responsibility early, first as charge nurse and then as a preceptor, and trusted me to grow into it. Six months into my career, I was training nurses who had more experience than I did. One of them was Diann, five feet tall, sharp-witted, nurturing and fierce all at once.

The first thing she said to me was, "Honey, I've been an ER nurse for eight years. What exactly do you think you're going to teach me?"

For a moment, I thought I might be sick. Instead, I smiled and said, "I'll show you where everything is, and you can show me how to use it."

That moment became my first true adult leadership lesson. Credibility does not come from pretending you know everything. It comes from owning what you do not. Diann raised me at the bedside, challenging me to lead with humility instead of ego. Over the years, she seemed to reappear just when I needed another lesson.

After several years in the ER and frequent visits to Suzie's office with ideas and opinions, she called me in and said, "You are the mouthiest, most opinionated ER nurse in this department with a bachelor's degree. I think you should apply for our new ER Nurse Educator position."

I resisted. I told her that if I moved to day shift, hospital administration would learn my name. I had chosen night shift to stay off the radar, especially after I had bypassed the chain of command and written directly to the CEO about safety concerns following the incident described earlier.

Suzie laughed. "Honey," she said, "they already know who you are."

She was right. That educator role became a turning point. There were no rigid parameters, only trust. I took frontline frustrations and turned them into onboarding improvements, just-in-time education, and practical systems that supported nurses in real moments of need. It was the first time I saw how influence could scale when paired with structure.

Eventually, I moved into a corporate clinical training role within organizational development, where I spent years deepening my understanding of adult learning, people development, management, and leadership influence. Those years gave language and framework to what I had intuitively practiced for a long time.

ER life hardened me in some ways and awakened me in others. After witnessing unimaginable trauma shift after shift, I eventually found my way to the ICU. Over the entrance hung a sign that read, "Quiet. Healing Environment." It felt like a different world. Leadership looked different there. Calmer. Slower. More deliberate.

In the ICU, I learned that leadership was not always about quick decisions. Sometimes it was about steady presence.

Around that same season, I met Rebecca, one of the most impactful leaders of my career and later my ICU director. Rebecca led with calm confidence and deep humanity. She understood that healthcare is a business - a profoundly human business. She taught me the art of timing, how to advocate and innovate without force, and how to collaborate rather than control.

The ICU taught me another hard truth. Emergency medicine had trained me to save everyone at any cost. The ICU revealed the weight of that philosophy. Sometimes survival comes with a price no one is prepared to pay.

The ICU also exposed trauma I had not fully acknowledged. Years of verbal and physical abuse in emergency medicine had conditioned my nervous system. When a patient's family member lunged toward me in gratitude, I ducked, convinced I was about to be struck. They were reaching out for a hug.

That moment changed me.

Leadership in the ICU required presence more than speed, listening more than fixing. It forced me to become a learner again and reminded me that lifelong learning is not a weakness, but a leadership strength.

Focused leadership seeks clarity.
Fearless leadership obeys the clarity it finds.

Entrepreneurship brought its own lessons, particularly through networking, mentorship, and community-building with local chambers of commerce. Heidi, with her creative brilliance and analytical precision, saw potential in me that I had not yet fully embraced. She challenged me to own my gift, sharpen my message, and grow into the leader she already believed I was.

Through nursing, trauma, crisis, mentorship, ministry, motherhood, and entrepreneurship, one theme became undeniable.

Focused and Fearless leaders are shaped by life long before they are shaped by classrooms.

From childhood chaos to ER nights, ICU revelations, entrepreneurial risks, mentors, chambers, and pandemic pressure, these experiences became the soil where Focused and Fearless Leadership took root.

You do not become a focused and fearless leader through titles or training alone. You become one by allowing life events to become leadership lessons and by choosing to learn from every one of them.

CHAPTER 1: FOCUSED & FEARLESS REFLECTIONS

"Focused leaders reflect on their past. Fearless leaders rise from it."

Which life events have shaped the leader you've become?

____

____

"Focused leaders see the pattern. Fearless leaders learn the lesson."

Where have you reflected, but not yet learned?

____

____

"Focused leaders seek clarity. Fearless leaders step into courage."

What part of your story is asking for clarity or courage today?

____

____

Focused leaders know what they don't know. Fearless leaders admit it, learn, and build credibility.

When in your career have you faced not knowing, not having needed knowledge? How did you deal with it? What could you have done to build (even) more credibility?

____

____

CHAPTER 02

The Power of Understanding People

"Focused leaders understand their style. Fearless leaders flex beyond it."

When I worked in organizational development, our leadership team regularly took managers, directors, and executives off-site for quarterly training. After one particular session, they returned buzzing with energy, laughing about "what color" everyone was and playfully labeling personality traits. At the time, it sounded more like entertainment than education.

Not long after, our manager recognized something important. As educators, we influenced hundreds of people across the organization, and if this framework was valuable for senior leadership, it might be worth exploring ourselves. She gathered our team and walked us through the True Colors assessment.

I found it interesting, but I will admit I was skeptical. Part of me wondered if it was simply a clever party trick, something fun but not particularly useful. Naturally, I decided to test the theory.

There was a human resources leader named Jeannie who, according to the assessment, was "gold." Gold personalities tend to be highly organized, detail-oriented, and most comfortable when they can prepare in advance. Jeannie and I had an ongoing dynamic. I did not see her often, but when I did, I was usually excited about a new idea and eager to share it.

The problem was timing.

The only place I ever seemed to run into Jeannie was the hospital cafeteria. She would rush in, grab her food, and head straight back to her office, always focused and clearly busy. Because those moments were rare, I would seize the opportunity and enthusiastically launch into whatever new idea I had, essentially cornering her while she tried to decide which direction to escape. Looking back, I probably resembled a small child chasing a very overstimulated cat.

After learning more about personality styles, I realized that if this framework held any real value, the way I approached Jeannie should matter.

So the next time she walked into the cafeteria and spotted me, I noticed the familiar hesitation. I caught up with her, greeted her warmly, and mentioned that I had a new idea I wanted to share. As expected, her shoulders visibly tensed, bracing for impact.

Then I changed tactics.

I paused and said, "It looks like you're really busy today. Why don't I make an appointment to meet with you next week and walk you through it then?"

Her body language immediately shifted. Her shoulders dropped. She smiled.

"That would be great, Melissa," she said. "You always have wonderful ideas. I'm slammed right now, but if you can schedule time on Friday, I'd love to hear what you've come up with." She then took the time to ask how my children were!

I walked away from that interaction knowing something important had just happened. Nothing about my idea had changed. What changed was how I communicated.

That moment was when I realized this work was not a gimmick. Understanding how people are wired, what they value, and how they process information has real implications for influence, trust, and effectiveness.

Before we dig into the deeper principles of Focused and Fearless Leadership, we must ground ourselves in a truth that affects every conversation, every relationship, and every team decision you'll ever make:

- People are wired differently.
- We think differently.
- We decide differently.
- We communicate differently.

And if we ignore those differences, we create misunderstandings, conflict, and unnecessary leadership emergencies.

Knowing how to lead only in your own preferred style leaves a lot of missed opportunities for influence on the table and also may cost you a few unnecessarily. Leadership isn't measured by your internal brilliance; it's measured by how effectively others can receive, understand, and respond to you. That means your ability to influence is directly tied to how well you understand people.

One of the most practical ways to build this awareness is through personality frameworks. Whether it's True Colors, DISC, The Elements, the Enneagram, Myers-Briggs, or even simple shape-based tests, most models point to four dominant tendencies people reflect in communication and behavior.

Below is the comparison chart I use when teaching leaders to quickly assess how someone prefers to think and communicate:

Translating Across Various Assessments

Key Characteristic	True Colors	DISC	The Elements
Organized Planner	Gold	Steadiness	Earth
Intense Visionary	Green	Dominance	Fire
Creative Free Spirit	Orange	Influence	Air
Harmonizing Communicator	Blue	Conscientiousness	Water

These categories are not boxes, they're lenses. They help you understand yourself, understand others, and remove the guesswork from communication. And yes, your personality shifts between environments. You might show up one way at work, another way with family, and yet another way in a faith or community setting. That doesn't make you inconsistent; it makes you human.

Knowing your style is Focused Leadership.
Flexing beyond it is Fearless Leadership.

It's one thing to think, "This is how I am."

It's another to ask, "How do THEY need me to communicate right now?"

This chapter walks through all four styles - how they show up, how they are misunderstood, and how to lead them well.

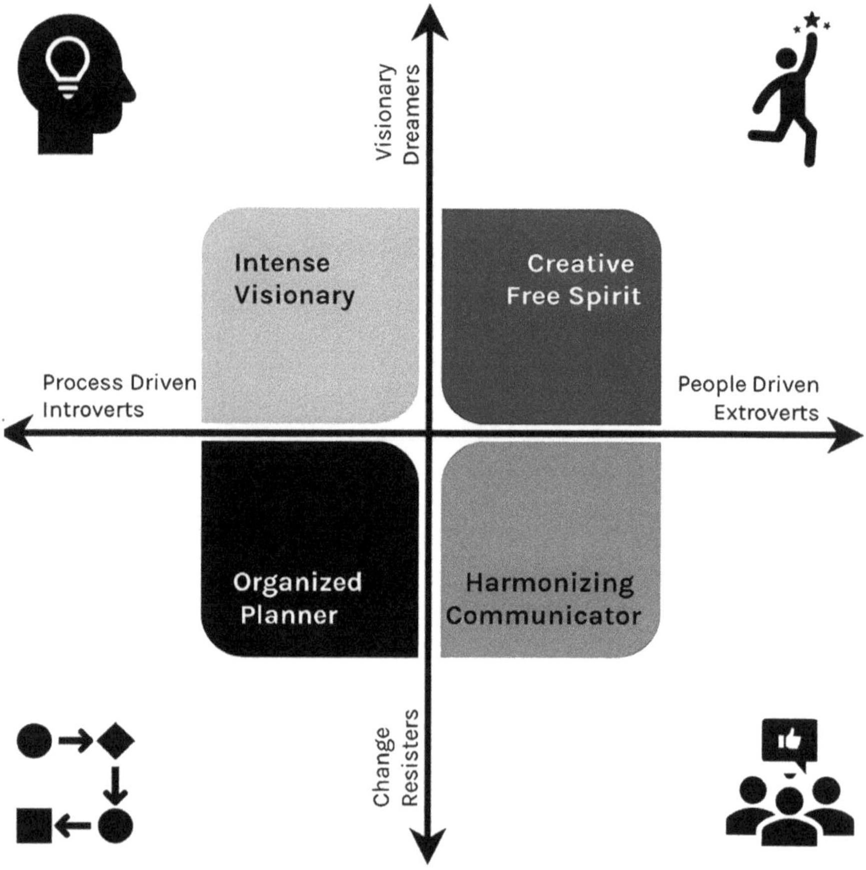

The Organized Planner

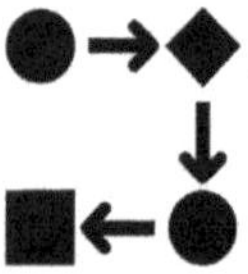

The Organized Planner is often introverted and deeply committed to order. If you were to step into their workspace, you would likely find everything intentionally placed. These are the people with multiple-colored pens and highlighters, carefully coding information so nothing is missed. They excel at sorting, organizing, and refining systems.

When an Organized Planner is working, their intensity can sometimes be misread. Their focused expression is often mistaken for frustration or irritation, when in reality they are simply concentrating. Many Organized Planners have heard jokes about "resting face," and while humor helps soften the moment, it can also lead to misunderstanding.

Organized Planners thrive in environments where things are clearly defined. They are most comfortable in black-and-white situations where decisions are framed as yes or no. One of their challenges is that they tend to gather data for a long time before deciding. Their desire to make the *right* decision can slow progress and frustrate others who prefer faster movement.

This personality is often labeled as obsessive or rigid, but what truly drives them is responsibility. Organized Planners are dependable, disciplined, and committed to doing things well. They value calm, structure, and follow-through. Because of this, they often struggle with rapid decision-making and unpredictable personalities. You will frequently find Organized Planners in professions that value accuracy and data, such as finance, compliance, and planning, guided by the belief that numbers tell the truth.

If asked to describe themselves, Organized Planners see themselves as stable and dependable. Timeliness matters to them, and being late feels like a personal failure. They take pride in being orderly, efficient, and reliable. They are realistic, goal-oriented, and committed to finishing what they start.

Without understanding this personality, others may perceive them as dull, rigid, opinionated, or bossy. They are often accused of being unable to multitask. In truth, they understand that multitasking reduces effectiveness, so they choose to focus instead.

For Organized Planners, growth comes from learning to make decisions with less information and taking calculated risks. Perfectionism can create unnecessary pressure, leading them to believe that mistakes erase credibility. Learning to tolerate imperfection builds resilience and adaptability, both essential for long-term leadership.

Those who work closely with Organized Planners should understand that their reserved nature is not a lack of warmth. Trust and respect must come first. Once those are established, you may find them more relaxed and even playful, though they are unlikely to be the loudest voice in the room.

The Intense Visionary

Across personality assessments, the Intense Visionary appears as Green in True Colors, Dominance in DISC, and Fire in The Elements. "Intense" is the most accurate word to describe them.

Intense Visionaries want the conclusion first. Once they understand the outcome, they can engage with the details. Without that clarity, they spend their energy trying to solve the ending rather than listening to the process. It is helpful to let them know upfront whether you are seeking a solution or simply a sounding board.

These individuals are logical, goal-driven, inventive, and highly competitive, often with themselves more than with others. They process information rapidly, analyzing cause and effect while others are still absorbing the basics. They are motivated by competence, innovation, and understanding the "why" behind decisions.

Because of this speed, Intense Visionaries can be perceived as disruptive. Their questions may feel abrupt or critical, even though they are simply thinking several steps ahead. They are rarely trying to dominate the room; they are trying to make sense of the system.

Intense Visionaries often remain calm during crises. Their strength lies in continuity and problem-solving under pressure. However, their intensity can lead to imbalance. Work often becomes their play, and they may fixate on a problem to the exclusion of everything else.

One of their greatest challenges is their critical nature. They set high standards and often raise the bar beyond what the organization originally intended. While excellence is admirable, this can lead to frustration when others are not operating at the same level. The person they are usually most critical of is themselves.

When describing themselves, Intense Visionaries often see creativity, precision, efficiency, and fairness as defining traits. They are strong advocates when injustice appears and will fiercely protect those who are marginalized.

Without understanding this personality, others may see them as intellectual snobs, emotionally distant, or overly critical. Intense Visionaries often recognize these perceptions and may even laugh about them.

Growth for the Intense Visionary requires awareness. There are moments when intensity is necessary, especially in a crisis. There are other times when that same intensity can alienate a team. Learning to modulate their approach allows their brilliance to be heard and respected.

They are also encouraged to rest, to step away, and to allow space for vulnerability. Admitting mistakes and showing humanity increases trust and expands influence.

The Creative Free Spirit

The Creative Free Spirit appears as Orange in True Colors, Influence in DISC, and Air in The Elements. They are dynamic, energetic, and driven by possibility.

Creative Free Spirits are vision-casters and innovators, often overflowing with ideas. They are skilled at problem-solving and thrive in environments with flexibility and creativity. Their challenge lies in execution. Structure, timelines, and follow-through can feel constraining.

Their greatest strength is adaptability, the ability to make something from nothing. Their greatest challenge is focus. Attention spans can wander, and rigid systems feel stifling. You often find Creative Free Spirits in artistic, entrepreneurial, or expressive professions.

They describe themselves as spontaneous, fun-loving, and capable of handling chaos. They prefer nuance and possibility over rigid answers.

Without understanding them, others may view Creative Free Spirits as flaky, irresponsible, or untrustworthy. Their natural ability to connect with others can sometimes be misinterpreted as manipulation, even though their intention is usually harmony.

Creative Free Spirits often help soften the Intense Visionary's edges by bringing attention back to people and influence. However, this can be misunderstood if communication is unclear.

Growth for this personality involves slowing down and becoming more intentional with communication. Speaking more deliberately, allowing others to finish thoughts, and resisting the urge to jump ahead creates stronger collaboration.

They are challenged to pause before making decisions and recognize when enthusiasm needs to be grounded in structure.

The Harmonizing Communicator

The Harmonizing Communicator appears as Blue in True Colors, Conscientiousness in DISC, and Water in The Elements. Their focus is people.

If asked to summarize themselves, they might say, "I'm here for you. What do you need?" They are empathetic, relational, and deeply committed to harmony.

Harmonizing Communicators are intuitive and perceptive, often reading emotional undercurrents before others notice them. They value authenticity and connection, and they work tirelessly to bring people together.

Their challenge is boundaries. Because they care deeply, they often say yes too often and neglect their own needs. Over time, this leads to exhaustion and resentment.

They may struggle in environments where strong hierarchy exists, preferring collaboration over authority. This can frustrate more directive personalities.

When misunderstood, Harmonizing Communicators may be seen as overly emotional, unrealistic, or naive. In reality, their compassion is a strength that requires protection.

Growth for this personality involves learning to say no, set boundaries, and hold others accountable. They must learn that honesty, even when uncomfortable, is an act of care.

Bringing It All Together

This overview offers only a glimpse into these four personalities. None is better than another. Each brings essential value to teams and organizations.

Through years of teaching and observation, I have noticed common friction points. Organized Planners and Creative Free Spirits often clash, much like north and south. Intense Visionaries and Harmonizing Communicators can feel like east and west, one pushing forward, the other slowing down to consider impact.

Most people are not one personality alone. We are blends. Who we are professionally may differ from who we are at home.

In my own leadership, I am a blend of the Intense Visionary and the Creative Free Spirit, full of ideas and passion, continually learning when to push forward and when to pause.

Learning to speak the language of all four personalities has transformed how I lead, coach, and build relationships.

You do not need to become someone you are not. You simply need to stop expecting everyone else to think, lead, and communicate exactly like you.

That is the work of a Focused and Fearless Leader.

CHAPTER 2: FOCUSED AND FEARLESS REFLECTIONS

"Focused leaders know their default style. Fearless leaders choose when to stretch."

Which personality style do you naturally lead with, and in what situations does it serve you well? Where does it limit your influence?

"Focused leaders recognize patterns. Fearless leaders adapt their approach."

**Think of a recent conflict or miscommunication.
Which personality styles were involved, and how could adapting your communication have prevented frustration or a "leadership emergency"?**

"Focused leaders value differences. Fearless leaders leverage them."

**Consider the people on your team (or in your circle).
Which styles are missing-or underrepresented?
How does that affect collaboration, creativity, or decision-making?**

"Focused leaders understand themselves. Fearless leaders see others clearly."

What assumptions do you make about other people's intentions or behaviors?
How might a personality-based explanation shift your perspective?

____

____

"Focused leaders communicate. Fearless leaders connect."

Where in your leadership can you slow down, listen better, or flex beyond your preferred style to create deeper rapport and stronger trust?

____

____

CHAPTER 03

The Power of Networking

"Focused leaders choose their circle. Fearless leaders grow it."

Leadership doesn't grow in isolation. It grows in circles; rooms, tables, and communities where we are seen, stretched, challenged, and supported. That's why networking is not just "nice to have" for entrepreneurs or executives; it is a strategic discipline for Focused and Fearless Leaders.

Focused leaders choose their circle with intention. Fearless leaders grow it by inviting new voices, new perspectives, and new opportunities into their world. One of the most powerful ways this has played out in my life is through networking, especially in my local Chamber of Commerce.

When I started MedicalTraining.me, several wise advisors told me, "If you're serious about this business, join your local Chamber." I didn't have many connections in the business community, so I took their advice. Looking back now, I can say without hesitation: my network has absolutely influenced my net worth, and not just financially. It has shaped my confidence, my opportunities, my collaborations, and even the way I see myself as a leader.

But that didn't happen overnight. When I first walked into rooms full of business owners, I felt completely out of place. Everyone seemed so polished and established. They knew each other's names, companies, and stories. They carried themselves with a level of ease I definitely did not feel.

My early attempts at networking were...rough. Maybe you'll recognize a few of these patterns in yourself.

The "I'm So Busy" Look

In those first events, my cell phone became my favorite accessory and my favorite hiding place. Any time I felt off balance or unsure of myself, I would scroll, swipe, or pretend to answer a message. It was easier to look busy than to risk standing alone or, worse, walking up to a group and not being welcomed in.

I only engaged with one or two people, and even then, I kept it safe and surface-level. The truth underneath it all was fear: What if I don't belong here? What if I'm not "enough" to be in this room?

Today, when I walk into a networking event, I intentionally look for the people I used to be-the ones standing on the margins, eyes on their phones, clearly uncomfortable. Yes, it would be easier to stay in my own comfortable circle of familiar faces, but Focused and Fearless Leadership calls me to something different. I feel a responsibility to cross the room, greet the newcomer, and help them feel seen. That's the Harmonizing Communicator in me-and it's also what growing your circle really looks like in practice.

The Drive-By Networking Approach

Once I realized the "busy" look wasn't helping, I upgraded (or so I thought) to what I now call the drive-by networking approach. My goal became to meet every single person in the room at least once. I measured success by the number of business cards I handed out and how many people I could tell about my company in one event.

Here's how it played out. I would:

- Walk up to someone with a big smile.
- Introduce myself and my business.
- Deliver a super-condensed version of my pitch.
- Hand over a card.
- Politely slide away to the next person.

Did it work? *Absolutely not.* Almost no one keeps a random stack of business cards from people they barely remember, especially if nothing specific stands out about the interaction or if they didn't clearly see the value you bring.

Over time, I learned that networking is not a numbers game; it's a relationship game. It's much more powerful to have three meaningful conversations than thirty shallow ones. Focused leaders slow down long enough to connect. Fearless leaders resist the hustle of "meeting everyone" and choose depth over breadth.

When possible, it helps to do your homework. Look at the attendee list, think about who you want to meet and why, and give yourself permission to stay in a conversation long enough to build rapport, not just exchange cards.

The "Look at Me" Approach

Once I abandoned the drive-by approach, I swung to the other extreme. I thought the solution was to become as interesting and memorable as possible, as quickly as possible. I crammed my entire story, my passion, my services, and my vision into the very first interaction.

You can probably guess how that went.

There were moments when I watched people literally lean back or subtly step away while I tried to "land the pitch" before they escaped. I wasn't trying to be pushy; I was just desperate to prove my value. But that desperation came across as pressure, and pressure rarely builds trust.

What I eventually realized is this: the first conversation is not the time to close the deal; it's the time to open the door. The goal of a first encounter is not to get someone to say "yes" to your offer. It's to create enough curiosity, trust, or connection that you both want there to be a second conversation.

Learning from the Queens (and Kings) of Networking

After striking out with all three of these approaches, I finally did what wise leaders do: I started studying the people who were clearly doing it well.

I listened more. I watched more. I paid attention to whose names kept coming up in conversations, and I heard things like, "You need to meet so-and-so; they know everyone and love to connect people." These were the people I quietly started to follow around the room (in a totally non-creepy, non-stalkerish way, of course) just to see how they operated.

One woman in particular stood out. She was a middle-aged professional who always looked polished and classy without being stuffy. She had an energy and smile that could light up a room. She seemed completely comfortable in her own skin. Sometimes I watched her in a very business-focused conversation. Other times, I saw her relaxed and more informal with people she clearly knew well.

As I observed her, I had this thought: "I bet she understands the different personalities too."

Here's what fascinated me most: I never heard her pitch her business. Not once. People knew her by name long before they could tell you the company she represented. That blew my mind. How could she be so successful and never be in "sales mode"?

The answer was simple but powerful: she was interested, not just interesting.

She spent most of the conversation listening. She asked real questions. She remembered details. She followed up. Her goal wasn't to close; it was to connect. When she genuinely believed two people needed to know each other, she made the introduction and in doing so, she quietly built tremendous influence.

Over time, she earned the kind of relational capital that allowed her to ask for what she needed without ever feeling pushy. Her network trusted her. That trust became its own form of net worth.

Your Network Influences Your Net Worth

Watching her and others like her taught me a critical pillar of Focused and Fearless Leadership:

- Your network influences your net worth.
- Not just in money, but in mentorship, wisdom, opportunity, and impact.

The people you surround yourself with shape how you think, what you see as possible, and how quickly you grow. Focused leaders choose their circle: they are intentional about spending time with people who are better, wiser, kinder, and more experienced in the areas they want to grow. Fearless leaders grow their circle: they consistently reach beyond the familiar to build bridges with people who don't look, think, or lead exactly like they do.

I share all of this to encourage you: networking is a learned skill. If you recognize yourself in any of my early mistakes, you're not broken; you're just in process. If I can go from hiding behind my phone and drive-by pitching to being seen as a connector and key networker, you can too.

I still talk too much sometimes. I still have to remind myself to slow down, ask better questions, and really listen. But I now see networking as part of my calling as a Focused and Fearless Leader. I seek to intentionally build circles where people feel seen, valued, and supported, and to create connections that outlive any single event.

CHAPTER 3: FOCUSED & FEARLESS REFLECTIONS

"Focused leaders notice their patterns. Fearless leaders disrupt them."

Which of the three approaches- "I'm So Busy," "Drive-By Networking," or "Look at Me" -do you tend to default to when you feel insecure in a room?

____

____

"Focused leaders know their wiring. Fearless leaders grow beyond it."

How can understanding your personality style (Organized Planner, Intense Visionary, Creative Free Spirit, Harmonizing Communicator) help you show up more authentically and confidently at networking events?

____

____

"Focused leaders drop what holds them back. Fearless leaders choose what moves them forward."

What bad networking habit do you need to drop so you can create more meaningful connections?

____

____

"Focused leaders curate their circle. Fearless leaders expand it with intention."

Who is one person you could intentionally invite into your circle this month -someone who challenges you, inspires you, or opens your perspective?

"Focused leaders influence their environment. Fearless leaders elevate everyone in it."

If you are already established in your organization or community, how can you use your influence to welcome newcomers, connect with others, and grow the circle for everyone?

> “ ***Focused leaders choose their circle.***
> ***Fearless leaders grow it.***

CHAPTER 04

Mitigation: The Crisis You Prevent

"Focused leaders identify risk early. Fearless leaders address it before it becomes an emergency."

In the mid-2000s, I participated in a full-scale countywide emergency preparedness drill involving four hospitals and a simulated dirty bomb explosion in an urban area. These drills are intentionally stressful, chaotic, and uncomfortable because real crises are exactly that.

The purpose is not to perform perfectly, it's to uncover the problems you *won't see* until you simulate pressure.

That day revealed many issues, but only one haunts me: The most knowledgeable person in the room stayed silent. Not because he lacked confidence. Not because he didn't know the right answer. Not because the situation overwhelmed him.

He stayed silent because he wasn't the "official leader." *(In a true event, this would have cost lives!)*

This single moment taught me more than any textbook. Unspoken hierarchy is a risk. Silence is a risk. Fear of "stepping out of place" is a risk. And mitigation must address human behavior and not just procedures. Emergency response is never just about rank, equipment or protocols.

It's about culture, communication, and courage.

Before alarms ring, before tensions spike, before the "big problem" becomes big... there are always signs. Subtle signs. Quiet signs. *Manageable* signs.

Every seasoned nurse, educator, executive, or parent knows: Emergencies rarely start as emergencies. They start as something small, something we excuse, overlook, or underestimate. Leadership emergencies follow this exact same principle.

Mitigation is the skill that separates leaders who merely *react* from leaders who respond to, *at best prevent it and at worst, manage it.* Mitigation is the art and discipline of seeing trouble before it mushrooms into a mess.

Understanding this one skill might save you years of frustration, unnecessary conflict, and preventable burnout.

The irony behind "Leadership Emergencies", the very premise of this book highlights a paradox. Most emergencies - medical, organizational, or personal - happen due to:

Lack of preparation, or

Lack of resources,

And often both simultaneously.

It's never the dramatic moment that causes the ultimate damage.

It's what *wasn't* done *before* it.

Early in my career, working as both a critical-care nurse and a Basic EMT, I learned this through hard-won experience. People often assume that successful emergency response is a heroic, adrenaline-filled moment.

But the truth?

Heroic responses only happen when preparation and resources collide at the exact right time. Without that, you get chaos, not courage.

Mitigation: The Invisible Phase of Leadership Most Leaders Skip

Mitigation is the first and most foundational stage of the emergency management cycle. Yet it's also the stage that feels the least urgent, which is precisely why it's the most overlooked.

Mitigation answers the question: "What could go wrong, and what are we doing about it now?" In emergency management, we use a formal tool: the Hazard Vulnerability Assessment (HVA).

Think of an HVA as the grown-up version of "What's the worst that could happen?" except written with data, probability, and honest assessment rather than denial, hope, or blind optimism.

An HVA forces you to evaluate:

- How likely a threat is
- What resources you have
- Where the gaps are
- How prepared you are to manage them

Hospitals run these assessments annually. And they are humbling.

For years, we confidently ruled out earthquakes in Eastern North Carolina. We laughed about it: *"Not us, not here."* And then... we felt one.

Life has a funny way of handing you reality checks.

Mitigation means updating your list based on what life has revealed, and not what you *thought* was true.

The Emergency Management Cycle, And Why Leaders Need It

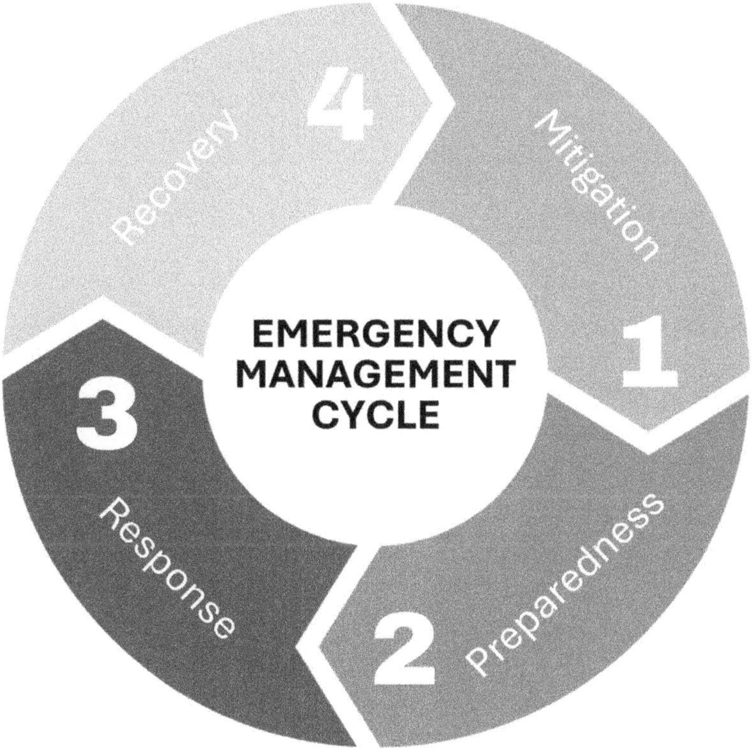

Emergency management isn't linear. It's a cycle, and leaders must treat it that way and respect the necessity of it.

1. **Mitigation**

   Identify risks/weaknesses (What is in our blind spot that we can now step back and see?)

   Study patterns of past lessons learned and other's shared experiences of how to strengthen systems and address weak spots

2. **Preparedness**

   Initiate the processes and training needs to decrease the likelihood of not having what you need in the moment.

   Practice/Simulate to test your solutions with an emphasis on role designation and building communication, as these are often the main pitfalls of any event (real or simulated).

3. **Response**

   Execute the plan or improvise, sometimes with duct tape, if you skipped the first two steps

4. **Recovery**

   Rebuild and restore stability. Debrief to identify successes and lessons learned. Establish the "new normal"

And then...it cycles back to mitigation. The same is true for your leadership.

Every argument, every missed deadline, every staff turnover, every breakdown in communication, every burned-out team member; every one of these moments teaches you something, *if* you're willing to ask:

- "What should this teach me next time?"

Most leaders don't ask. Focused and fearless leaders do.

Your Life Has an HVA, Even If You've Never Written It Down

Every leader has a personal hazard vulnerability profile that covers potential crises that can occur in their world:

- The coworker whose frustration keeps simmering
- The project nobody has fully defined
- The uncomfortable conversation you keep postponing
- The system you've outgrown and/or become outdated but haven't rebuilt
- The team member underperforming, because they're overwhelmed
- The communication habit that always gets you in trouble
- The boundaries you haven't set
- The resentment you haven't voiced
- The exhaustion you keep pushing through

These are your version of "earthquakes" and "dirty bomb drills."

Mitigation a Superpower?

Mitigation means facing what you've been hoping will magically resolve itself.

Hint: It won't.

"Focused leaders identify risk early"
"Fearless leaders address it before it becomes an emergency."

Mitigation means not being surprised by what humans do under pressure.

Mitigation acknowledges the truth: No system usually breaks because of one moment. Systems break because warning signs were ignored.

The Critical Question Every Leader Must Ask

Before any crisis arrives, ask: "What problem have I ignored/ tolerated too long?"

Leadership emergencies are rarely sudden. Like snowballs, they are slow accumulations of ignored information. And the longer something is tolerated, the more dramatic the issue becomes.

Mitigation is the leadership superpower that decreases the likelihood of heroics ever being needed.

Leaders who mitigate well:

CHAPTER 4: FOCUSED & FEARLESS REFLECTIONS

"Focused leaders spot the signs. Fearless leaders act before they ignite."

When you look at your team or organization right now, what small warning signs (friction, silence, delay, avoidance) are signaling a risk you've been overlooking?

____

____

"Focused leaders learn from the past. Fearless leaders adjust for the future."

What recent experience, mistakes, or near-miss should now inform your personal or organizational mitigation plan?

____

____

"Focused leaders notice quiet voices. Fearless leaders create space for them."

Who holds insight, awareness, or expertise that is going unheard? How can you make sure their voice prevents your next crisis?

____

____

"Focused leaders acknowledge vulnerabilities. Fearless leaders confront them."

What system, habit, or behavior has hinted at trouble? And what conversation, boundary, or decision is now calling for courage?

____

____

"Focused leaders see the risk. Fearless leaders reduce it."

What is one action-simple, strategic, or overdue-you can take this week to lower preventable risk for yourself, your team, or your organization?

____

____

CHAPTER 05

How Humans Respond in Crisis

"Focused leaders know their wiring. Fearless leaders regulate and work beyond it."

I am reminded of a time when I was involved in a training by Active Threat Solutions trauma medical/stop the bleed class that included an active shooter scenario. It was a fascinating class, and as much as I knew about trauma and skills, I still learned an incredible amount about the content and myself as it was designed to teach learners how to respond until help and resources arrived. The two-day training culminated in a full-blown drill that really drove the points home and allowed us to use the skills we had learned. Because of my experience, I decided that I wanted to be in the first round of responders as they separated the class and repeated the drill in small groups three or four times.

This training was held at a small rural Baptist church, and most of the attendees were members of this church. Our team of four providers included me, a young woman interested in EMS, a woman who was in the middle of Basic Law Enforcement Training (BLET), and another attendee whose purpose for being there has long been forgotten.

The drill began with little to no warning. We heard some men arguing, and I heard a gun fired at least three times. A man began screaming and off we went. One girl called 911 to report the incident, and we tried to figure out if the scene was safe as we approached the fellowship hall door. I think the BLET woman was the one with a gun clearing the scene, but just like in real life, details in certain portions are hard to recall.

I do remember after we entered, there was a man sitting against the wall screaming. He had a gunshot wound (GSW) to his left leg, and he was yelling for help and cursing about the shooter. We asked him where the shooter was, and he said they had left the building. The EMS girl went over to him to start assessing his wound while he was yelling about the "son of a bitch that shot my buddy" who was in another area out of view. He kept calling for the man, but no one was responding.

In this moment, I learned a valuable insight about myself which was quite unexpected. Remember, your fight-or-flight response is instinctual. I learned that if I have help with me and someone in need is loud and overwhelming, with a team of responders, I am more likely to let others intervene first. My rationale: they obviously have an airway if they can yell, which is a great thing, and someone else can start to manage the rest of the assessment. I am more likely to find the next person who needs help and intervention, which is exactly what I did. I never knew this about myself until this event. I assumed that because I had years of experience with stress and trauma, I would tune out the extraneous factors and focus on what was needed.

I was surprised to see that my response was somewhat rattled during this event. Later, during our debriefing, and many times on my own, I replayed the experience in my mind and analyzed how my response was different in my non-clinical environment. Not being in a mindset of readiness/preparedness really shifted my response. I also think that if I had been alone and they were the first victim I found, I would have stopped to finish a basic assessment for the life-threatening injuries.

Because someone was there to help the yelling man, I went to the adjacent kitchen area and found the second victim unresponsive. I began my assessment as we had been taught and quickly found a neck wound from the gunshot. I immediately applied pressure to control the bleeding. This was when the two other team members came into the room. I told the BLET girl to start reassessing, because when I was doing the quick assessment for bleeding, his pants felt moist. I didn't notice obvious bleeding, and the neck wound took my attention. She began with his legs and immediately found bleeding in his left groin area. As she removed his pants, a spray of blood shot out from the femoral artery. Without even thinking, I put my finger in his wound and manually occluded the bleed. I was in a surreal state and quickly realized my left hand was holding his neck wound, and my index finger was literally in his groin bullet wound. I remember looking at the wounds and my hands a couple of times before realizing, "Melissa, delegate!"

In my focused response, I took complete control, thus having one hand on his neck to control bleeding and my right index finger buried in a bullet wound in his thigh, where I could feel the artery compress when I pushed on it to stop the bleeding. This is great for bleeding control, but now I was literally out of hands. The victim needed more help, but if I let go of either area, the bleeding would return. How many times in life do we forget to look up and grab the bystanders who can help when we are frozen in the moment of surrealism?

The EMT girl had come in by this time, so I asked her if she felt comfortable taking over wound care of the neck, to which she quickly responded that she was. The BLET girl didn't look so great, but she was hanging in there. She wasn't comfortable managing this arterial bleed, so I delegated the supplies I needed, and she did a great job of assisting me while I packed the wound. It was intense. I was trying to catch my breath and reassess the situation when I was told that the patient was still in respiratory distress.

If this scenario is intense for you, take a breath and remember this is a training exercise, and this victim is a 200-pound lifelike manikin. It definitely triggered my focus, fold, or freeze response and felt very real. I kept performing basic airway and breathing interventions that didn't work and was told I didn't have the tools I wanted to use on the patient, which left me feeling angry and frustrated. My head was literally pounding, and I could feel my pulse in my ears. I realized I must have missed a wound. I quickly rechecked the victim and found a gunshot wound in the armpit/chest area.

I later learned it was called the "Ronald Reagan" because of the injury Regan received when he was shot in the 80s. I immediately applied a one-way valve occlusive dressing. This intervention stabilized the victim, and EMS was finally on the scene to take over care. With this, the drill ended successfully.

Now, as an educator, I can tell you that the hands-on portion of this was crucial because of the application of skills learned, the personal insight gained, and the ability to debrief with professionals who were watching our response the entire time. It was invaluable and something I will never forget. In fact, because I see the value of this specific trauma training (after taking the course several times myself) and the need to work through the very real fight or flight response that happens in this type of crisis, I recently acquired this company's training to continue the great work they began ten years ago.

Before we talk about leading others through a crisis, we have to understand something more fundamental: how humans instinctively react when they feel threatened.

Your nervous system does not distinguish the trigger of frustration/rage due to a traffic jam versus the fear of a dinosaur attempting to eat you. It simply reacts.

Years ago in disaster preparedness training, the speaker said that in a crisis when our nervous system is triggered, we typically respond in one of three ways: focus, fold, or freeze. The concepts of focus, fold, and freeze are grounded in trauma and nervous system research, particularly Stephen Porges's Polyvagal Theory, which explains how the body responds under threat before conscious thought occurs (Porges, 2011).

Enhanced Stress Response Framework

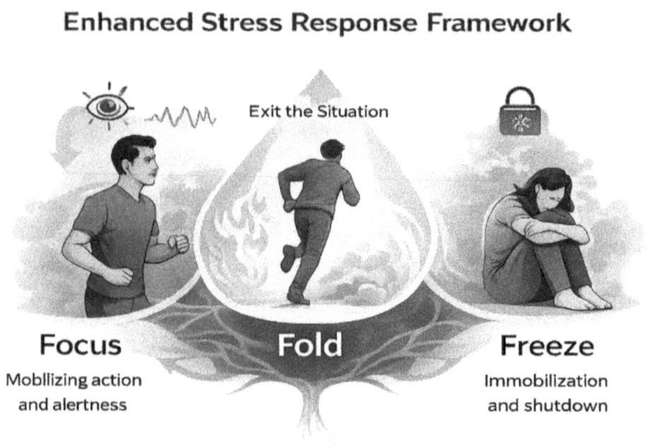

Focus: People who are focused will jump in and respond to the emergency but may have tunnel vision that blocks their need to delegate to other bystanders who seem to watch but do not get involved. This is actually called the "bystander effect" and happens quite commonly.

Fold: People who fold will pass out, vomit, or run away screaming to escape the crisis. Their self-preservation mode is in overdrive, and their adrenaline pushes them to a place of perceived safety.

Freeze: People who freeze are the ones who stand there watching without responding. It's like driving past a bad car crash and not being able to look away even though you know what you are witnessing is not okay. The bystander effect has been proven to occur most often when individuals in a group do not help someone in need.

We typically fall into one of these three categories for most situations, so it's crucial to consider this as you work to become a leader and influencer. Think of the last time something especially intense happened: how did you respond?

Now, don't get me wrong. We all respond in all three ways. I have definitely had moments where I thought, "Damn, Melissa, you knew what to do, so why didn't you offer to help?" (e.g., someone struggling with a projector issue while giving a talk).

The Human Response to Perceived Threat

I've shared this story to introduce a few more critical concepts about how we respond to leadership emergencies (often without realizing it).

Our bodies scan the environment for safety up to five times every second. When a real or potential threat is detected, the body responds the same way either way. It does not pause to determine intent. It simply asks, *"Am I safe?"*

That's why we instinctively evaluate interactions using what Michael Bungay Stanier describes as the T.E.R.A. model (*The Coaching Habit*, pp. 121–122):

T – Tribe: Are the others involved for me or against me?
E – Expectation: Do I know what's coming?
R – Rank: Does this person hold power over me?
A – Autonomy: Will I get a say in the outcome?

This is powerful information for any leader or influencer. It reminds us that how we approach people matters just as much as what we say - especially when offering feedback, whether positive or corrective.

As I've used this framework in my communication as a business owner, community leader, healthcare professional, and even as a parent, I've come to realize two important things:

First, this response is universal and happens whether the threat is real or perceived.

Second, there is one critical factor that consistently intensifies threat when it's mishandled.

So, I add two more letters refining the language to reflect what's fully happening in the nervous system.

Together, these elements form what I call the **THREAT** response.

The THREAT Response

T - Tribe
Are the others involved for me or against me?
Who's in the room? Who's copied to the email? Who already knows? Tribe determines trust before a meeting happens or even before a word is ever spoken.

H - Hierarchy
Does this person hold power, authority, or influence over me?
Hierarchy acknowledges real-world dynamics without judgment. Power exists whether we name it or not.

R - Reliability
Can I trust the leader and the process?
Uncertainty fuels anxiety. Clarity builds safety. Reliability reduces the need for self-protection.

E - Empowerment
Will I have a voice or meaningful influence in the outcome?
People don't need control, but they do need to feel understood and heard.

A - Anticipation

Can I predict what's coming?

Waiting often creates more stress than the conversation itself.

T - Timing

How soon will this happen AND when will it be over?

Timing doesn't just affect schedules; it affects psychological safety.

A vague request to "talk later" without context can trigger focus, fold or freeze before the conversation even begins. This is why a leader who says:

"We need to talk Monday morning.
Have a good weekend."

...is an emotional terrorist. Not intentional. But absolutely avoidable.

If your message feels like a THREAT, it won't be heard no matter how well it's intended. Instead ensure clear and SAFE communication

Why THREAT Triggers Leadership Emergencies

A perceived threat, to what we know, what we believe in and/or what we can control, activates the nervous system just as powerfully as a real physical danger. The response is the same whether the threat is real or imagined.

The result is *Focus, Fold, or Freeze*. This is not a character flaw. It is human physiology.

Focused leaders recognize this.
Fearless leaders adjust their approach, so they don't activate it in others.

When leaders ignore THREAT, people protect themselves. When leaders manage THREAT, people collaborate.

Why This Matters for Leadership

Every preventable crisis has a moment, sometimes loud, but often small and silent, when someone feels: Unsafe/Unseen/Unsure/Unheard. We have all felt it in that tense staff meeting or from the employee who suddenly pulls away. Remember that time you didn't think that conflict was a big deal? How about that time that the "quick announcement" that spiraled into panic.

These are not personality defects. They are primitive nervous-system responses.

Focused & Fearless Leadership begins with recognizing three things at the same time:

Your wiring

Their wiring

The signs of a triggered event

Because leaders don't just manage problems. They manage human physiology which can be unpredictable.

Leadership emergencies happen when we forget this. And this is exactly why *how* we set up communication matters just as much as *what* we plan to say.

Reducing THREAT Before the Conversation Begins

One of the most effective ways to prevent unnecessary threat activation is to be intentional *before* the meeting ever starts. In my Masterclass work, I challenge leaders to use the SAFE Communication Framework when setting up conversations-especially those involving feedback, uncertainty, or change. SAFE is not about avoiding hard conversations. It's about lowering the THREAT response so those conversations can actually be productive.

S: Set Up the Meeting

Set the conditions for safety before the conversation begins.

- Share **time**, **context**, and **intended outcome**
- Remove unnecessary surprises
- Let people know what the meeting *is* and *is not*

As mentioned earlier, uncertainty fuels imagination. Our instinctual imagination often assumes danger.

A: Acknowledge Uncertainty / Allay Concerns / Announce the Topic

Name what others may already be feeling.

- Normalize discomfort
- Signal intent
- Clarify what is open for discussion and what is not

A simple script might sound like: *"I want to talk about X. I don't have all the answers, but I want your honest input on how we improve."*

Clarity reduces threat. Silence amplifies it.

F: Fight-or-Flight Mitigation

Once the conversation begins, your presence matters. 80% of communication is said in body language. People take cues from your nervous system before they process your words.

- Relaxed body language
- Slower and lower tone of voice
- Neutral, curious questions
- Remember under stress, someone hears about 20% of what was said.

E: Explain Expectations / Emotional Regulation

Close the loop.

- Tell people what will happen with their input
- Share the timeline for follow-up
- Reduce ambiguity about next steps

When people know what to expect, their nervous system can reset.

The Leadership Truth

When leaders ignore THREAT, people protect themselves. When leaders use SAFE communication, people stay engaged, even when conversations are hard. This is not about being soft. It's about being strategic. Because leadership isn't just about saying the right thing, it's about creating the conditions where the right thing can actually be heard.

> "*Focused leaders recognize the moment threat appears. Fearless leaders adjust their approach, so they don't activate it unnecessarily.*"

CHAPTER 5: FOCUSED & FEARLESS REFLECTIONS

"Focused leaders recognize their triggers. Fearless leaders prepare for them."

What situations, conversations, or people tend to activate your threat response?

____

____

"Focused leaders pause before reacting. Fearless leaders choose their response."

Where is one place in your leadership where a 10-second pause could change everything?

____

____

"Focused leaders understand human nature. Fearless leaders create psychological safety."

How might you unintentionally trigger T.H.R.E.A.T. response in others-and what can you adjust?

____

____

"Focused leaders know their wiring. Fearless leaders regulate it."

Which instinct-Focus, Fold, or Freeze-shows up first for you when stress spikes?

____

____

"Focused leaders manage the moment. Fearless leaders lead the environment."

What is one way you can lower the emotional temperature of your workplace this week?

____

____

CHAPTER 06

Communication & Collaboration Under Pressure

"Focused leaders communicate with intention. Fearless leaders collaborate for solutions."

Early in my leadership career, my organizational development director pulled me into her office. She asked me if I had ever considered whether there was ever more than one solution to any given problem. I quickly shot back, "No. If you figure out the answer, why would you waste your time?" Remember, I was just coming out of an ER nursing career where we made quick decisions, often without the luxury of debate or consideration. She initially looked shocked, which let me know very quickly that I was wrong. I took a breath and waited for her judgment or criticism, and I was pleasantly relieved. Instead of condemning me and saying that she made a mistake in hiring me, she began to share her thoughts.

My inner critic had been so quick to respond and so very harsh. If you think of this related to the Thomas-Kilmann Conflict Modes, my director had options for how to manage me. If she had been less confident, less experienced, or just not in the mood to work with me, she could have quickly contended with me. If she were contending, she would have said, "Well there is and you need to keep your mouth shut. And if you can't do that, then I will fire you." It would have worked (for a minute), but if she had behaved like this, I would have quickly done what she said, but I also would have lost respect for her as my leader and then would have been looking for my next job. Instead, my director chose to collaborate with me.

She simply asked how many committees I sat on in the hospital. I shocked her when I told her that I sat on 13. She then asked who came up with most of the solutions, and I quickly responded that it was me. She then asked, "Melissa, who has to come up with the processes to apply the solutions?" I began to see her point as I responded, "Dang, it's usually me." She then asked, "If you had to wait and share your response, would your thought expire?" I laughed and said, "Well, no, but I may explode while waiting for others to figure out the obvious." She laughed and said, "I have a challenge for you. We are about to go into our division meeting. I want you to wait at least 30 seconds, more if you can handle it, before you respond to my questions. I want you to observe what happens with the team." I shook my head while laughing and agreed, as she's my director; am I really going to not accommodate her? There's an example for you!

I went into the meeting and did as she asked. It was amazing. Slowly, others started speaking up, and some even had the same ideas as me. As they talked, I was able to take their ideas and combine them with mine to create an even better solution. That was the day I truly and consciously learned the value of collaboration. I went back to her office excited to discuss it all. I told her I was amazed at how many people not only got involved but also got excited. I shared that it was painful at first to stay quiet, but as I saw others contribute, it was intoxicating to witness how everything went into motion. She smiled and thanked me for indulging her.

I thought the lesson was over, and then she shared this with me: "Melissa, I called you in and had this conversation because

I was you 20 years ago when my career began. I understand your passion, and it took someone stepping on my toes a bit to help me grow too." I gained immense respect for her as a leader in our organization, and this made me buy into working under her leadership even more. I obviously had a lot to learn.

This is an excellent story about how collaboration leaves everyone winning. She got a better employee out of me, as I grew so much from that conversation, which then benefited our team. I grew in respect for her and began to look to her as a role model in how to manage others. That lesson was learned almost 20 years ago and I still talk about it, which is the kind of leadership impact I want to have on others.

Why Communication Breaks Down in Leadership Emergencies

Most leadership emergencies don't begin with a major error. They begin with a misunderstood email, a tone taken the wrong way, a hesitation to speak up, or a leader who reacts instead of responds.

Conflict isn't the problem.

Unskilled communication durin conflict is.

In healthcare, business, and community leadership alike, I've seen teams unravel not because they lacked the knowledge but because they lacked the skill, composure, and confidence to communicate under pressure. That's why this chapter focuses on *how* leaders show up when stakes rise and how to do it with purpose rather than panic.

The Five Ways Leaders Respond to Conflict (Thomas – Kilmann Model)

Conflict modes are instinctive patterns we fall into when emotions spike. They shape every difficult conversation, every team disagreement, and every leadership emergency. The Thomas-Kilmann Conflict Resolution Modes (Thomas and Kilmann 1974, 2-3) is a great concept to review. It explains that depending on how assertive you are (your willingness to stand up for yourself) and also how cooperative you are (your willingness to push back when someone is being unkind), you will choose one of five representations:

1. **Contenders** are the most assertive and uncooperative people. Contenders don't care about anything except getting their way in that moment.
2. **Accommodators** are the polar opposite of contenders. They are not aggressive at all and are totally cooperative. They just want conflict to be quickly resolved.
3. **Withdrawers** are the least cooperative or aggressive. They simply pretend that conflict doesn't exist and hope it goes away.
4. **Compromisers** are willing to give up some of what they want in order to get at least part of what they desired. They are assertive and cooperative; thus, I thought this was the most effective way to resolve conflict, but I had forgotten about the last one.
5. **Collaborators** are the most assertive and cooperative, as they choose to meld their ideas with others in order to come up with a solution where everyone wins.

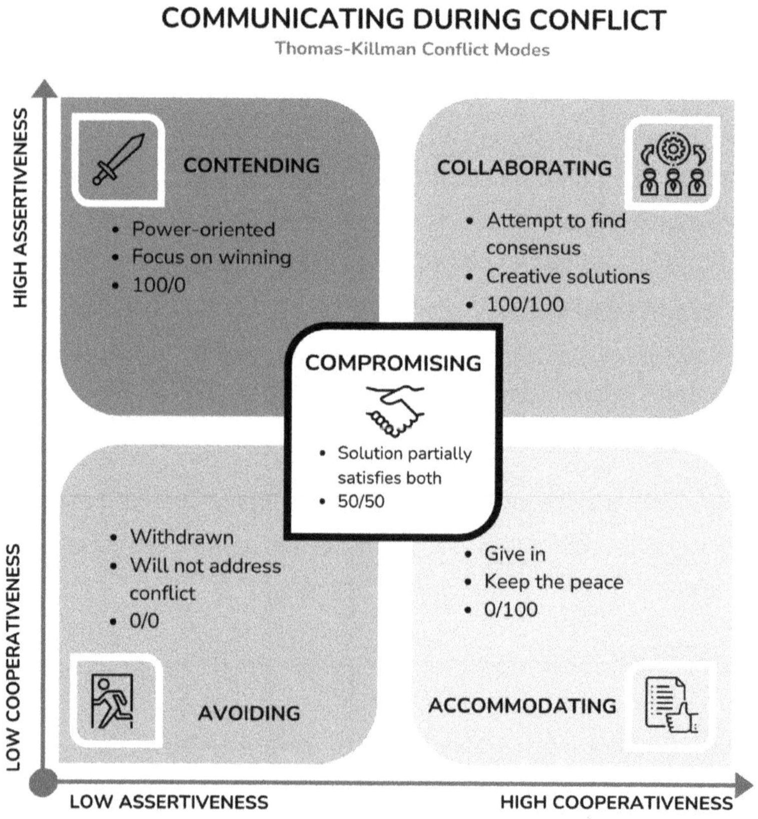

Similar to the Focus, Fold, or Freeze information, I thought that I would only use one way to resolve conflict, which is my natural inclination to collaborate. I ate some humble pie when I reflected on how I had handled some situations in the past. Think back to my initial response in the active shooter drill. I definitely avoided the first victim who was yelling and cursing. I then transitioned into a contending role as I intervened, and the others arrived to assist me. As they engaged, I would like to believe that we collaborated quite well, but it definitely wasn't my first response, and rightfully so.

If you are not a medical professional, don't feel left out or that this doesn't apply. This same response is used anytime a threat approaches, so this could just as easily be a disgruntled co-worker or an irate customer. Or even worse, it could be a family member who knows which buttons to push in order to send you over the edge.

Contenders

When it comes to recognizing and understanding response styles, I think of that song "All I Do is Win, Win, Win, No Matter What..." by DJ Khaled. Contenders don't care what others think; it's their way or no way. I would dare to say that a lot of leaders in the 80s and early 90s used this technique, which I affectionately refer to as the "do it or heads will roll" mentality. And it can work until it doesn't. Eventually, people will get fed up with domination and begin to question the leader's abilities and push back. Now, don't get me wrong; there are times to contend, as in the active shooter role. The most obvious reason is when safety is involved, and life and death hang in the balance. It is often the only way to respond, so we must be honest and say, "Yes, there have been times when this was my initial response."

Accommodators

Next, let's look at accommodation, as it often works in tandem with contention. Accommodators will give up and give in; they get nothing in return. They are often labeled as human doormats. They give in 100 percent of the time. My initial thought about this type of resolution was that it was too weak, but after reflection, I realized there are times when accommodation is a great thing. When the stakes are low or it really doesn't matter to me, I may choose to accommodate the other person.

I view both personal and professional relationships like bank accounts. For a bank account to exist, deposits must be made so that withdrawals can be taken later. In a relationship, sometimes you accommodate to make a deposit into the account to build goodwill and prepare for other times when you may need to withdraw on a bigger issue. It's just part of being a good human being.

Withdrawers

The withdrawing avoiders (least cooperative and least accommodating) bury their heads in the sand and wait for things to blow over. This style drives me the craziest. How do you find resolution if someone "checks out?" But then, upon reflection, there are times when we need to actively avoid. Most commonly, we should avoid when emotions are high, the stakes are high, and resolution of any sort will not happen without unnecessary destruction.

Again, in critical care, we are taught situational awareness. Situational awareness is scanning the environment to ensure safety and anticipate if someone may be a threat. In critical care training, we are taught to stand between the person and the exit so that if things escalate and we are unable to manage the crisis, we can "de-ass the premises," meaning to leave the area for another place of safety until the crisis is de-escalated.

Imagine you are an ER nurse giving someone devastating news. This triggers them, which causes their fight/flight (focus/fold/freeze) response to fire. Most people are grief-stricken and emotional, but I have seen many times where the initial response was violence. They may hit a wall or pick something up to throw. These are excellent times to withdraw if you cannot quickly interrupt this reaction.

Most of you reading this book are not in critical care, so these examples may feel extreme, but I often share them in my non-medical leadership training because they help demonstrate a point. Non-medical workplace events can also apply when someone is angry due to a coworker not pulling their weight or an angry client wanting a refund.

Compromisers

The last two modes - compromise and collaboration - are similar in that both parties are participating and will win. Before looking at this model closely, I would have believed that compromise was the most successful, but it's not. With compromise, each party gains something, but they also have to give something up. This becomes necessary when it's the only way to resolve the issue. Think of political parties that want their bills passed, but the other side really doesn't want it. There's always some kind of "you owe me" moment when the bill is modified to include components unrelated to the original intent, and the original bill has to be modified to remove original components. This is why I would make a terrible politician. I too quickly call bullshit on this type of stuff, as it infuriates me. It makes me feel slimy and taken advantage of. BUT that being said, there are times when you must compromise. It's a painful and necessary reality, even if only a temporary solution.

Collaborators

Finally, we have my FAVORITE: collaboration. This occurs when both parties want to be assertive and work together to form a better plan than either side could create alone. This FUELS my fire all the time. But let me tell you, I have had some real-life lessons to learn about collaboration as well.

Why Communication Can Still Fail

Communication does not fail because leaders lack intelligence, good intentions, or experience. It fails when leaders are **unfocused in how they listen** and **fearful of what they might hear**.

Focused and fearless leaders understand something many miss. Communication is not about transmitting information. It is about creating the conditions where the *best thinking in the room* can surface and the best ideas are shared. When those conditions are absent:

- Strong ideas stay silent,
- Collaboration erodes, and
- Preventable problems quietly grow into leadership emergencies.

I learned this lesson early (and personally).

Remember my story earlier about Jeannie in the cafeteria? I was always so excited to share a newest epiphany/idea with her. I had energy, clarity, and confidence. What I didn't have was awareness. Jeannie's personality style (Organized Planner) preferred structure and preparation. My spontaneous enthusiasm felt less like collaboration and more like ambush.

Nothing about the idea changed. What changed was my approach.

The next time, I asked to schedule a meeting. The relief on her face told me everything I needed to know. She even paused to asked how my kids were doing. That was the moment I realized this work wasn't a hat trick, it's real AND effective.

Focus creates access.
Fearlessness creates space.

Years later, I saw the same dynamic play out at a much higher level.

I accompanied a mentor to a conversation with a high-profile leader exploring leadership consulting. The moment they entered the room; their presence filled it. They exuded confidence, authority, and certainty. When asked to describe their challenge, they shared their frustration: their team showed up to meetings but never spoke. No ideas. No questions. No engagement. My mentor asked how meetings were structured.

The leader explained they sent an agenda in advance, which initially sounded promising. Then they added, "And with that agenda, I explain what we'll discuss and exactly why we should do what I think should be done." The barrier became immediately clear. This leader was fearless in certainty but unfocused on invitation. The meeting wasn't designed for collaboration; it was designed for compliance. The conversation was over before it began.

We shared how small shifts in communication could increase engagement, strengthen culture, and even improve retention. We learned the organization had a growing number of open positions and quietly connected leadership style to instability. They chose not to pursue the work. The culture didn't change. Eventually, that leader, known for being exacting and rigid, fell from grace and no longer leads. It was a loss. Their talent and intelligence were exceptional, but their leadership lacked the balance of focus and fearlessness required to sustain trust.

The Hidden Variable: How People Process

In *Radical Candor*, Kim Scott (2017, 75-104) describes loud listeners and quiet listeners, language that gave structure to something I had already been practicing instinctively.

Loud listeners process externally. Speaking *is* thinking. Ideas are drafts, not declarations.

Quiet listeners process internally. They reflect first, speak later, and often wait until their thoughts feel complete.

When loud listeners speak confidently and quickly, quiet listeners often assume decisions have already been made and their valuable insight is never shared.

Focused and fearless leadership reframes this entirely. The power is not in labeling people as loud or quiet. The power is in choosing how to listen with intention and ensure an environment that solicits all feedback, which sometimes means intentionally calling on a quiet listener to encourage participation.

The LENS Framework: Listening for Collaboration

To help leaders collaborate more effectively-while respecting both loud and quiet communicators, I teach the **LENS Framework**.

L: Look for Alignment
Before responding, notice where values, goals, or concerns already overlap. Alignment builds safety and momentum.

E: Engage Curiously
Replace certainty with curiosity. Ask questions that invite thinking, not defense.

N: Notice Patterns and Variance
Who speaks quickly? Who waits? Who hasn't spoken at all? Silence and speed both carry information.

S: Speak Up

Leaders model the behavior they want. Loud processors name their process. Quiet processors contribute earlier, even when ideas feel unfinished.

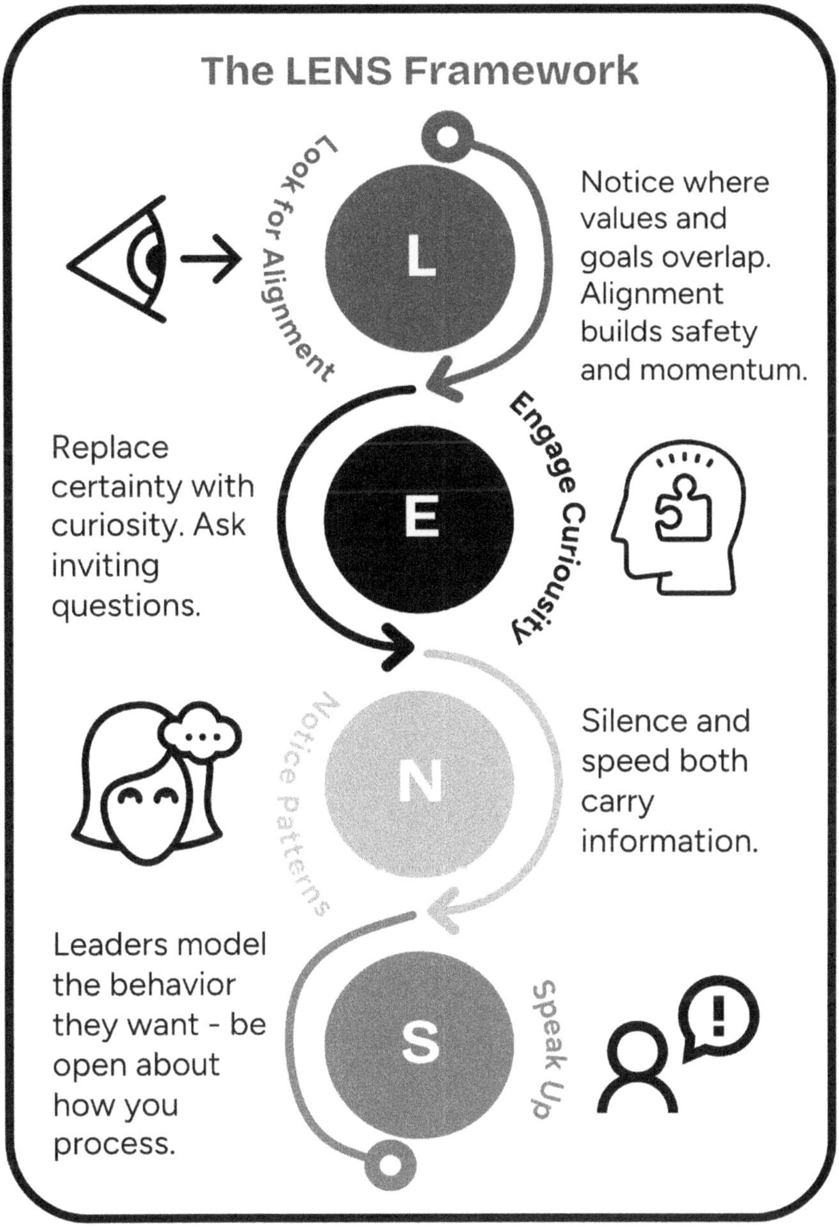

When leading a meeting, because I am an aloud thinker, often sounding determined and convinced, I often say:

"I'm thinking aloud. Please tell me what I'm missing, how this could be better, or why it won't work."

That single sentence does a few focused and fearless things to invite feedback.

- It slows the room
- It lowers defensiveness
- It signals that courage is welcome

Over time, I realized this wasn't a personality trait. It was a leadership discipline.

Focused and fearless leaders don't default to instinct. They lead with *intention*.

That means loud listeners should pause or at least slow down, name their process, and invite dissent. Quiet listeners speak earlier, even when certainty feels incomplete.

Leaders replace certainty with curiosity. Teams learn that disagreement is contribution, not conflict. When leaders consistently create space for both loud and quiet communicators, ideas improve, ownership increases, and crises are prevented long before they appear.

Focused and fearless leadership doesn't eliminate mistakes. It creates the culture that allows teams to recover, adapt, and grow together. And it begins with listening on purpose.

CHAPTER 6: FOCUSED & FEARLESS REFLECTIONS

"Focused leaders speak with clarity. Fearless leaders listen with intention."

Which conflict mode do you instinctively default to- Contend, Accommodate, Withdraw, Compromise, or Collaborate?

____

____

"Focused leaders regulate their tone. Fearless leaders regulate their impact."

How do you show up when conversations get tense-loud, quiet, reactive, analytical, guarded, or emotional?

____

____

"Focused leaders create space. Fearless leaders share it."

If you're a loud listener, how can you create more room for others?
If you're a quiet listener, what would it look like to take up more space?

____

____

CHAPTER 07

Authenticity: Leading Without a Mask

"Focused leaders show up real. Fearless leaders show up whole."

From my perspective, here's what I was thinking before that Zoom business meeting:

- *These are influential people. Don't waste their time.*
- *You're still new in this role. Be professional. Earn their respect.*
- *You're a small business owner in a room full of larger organizations. You need to show you belong here.*

I wanted to be seen as an Organized Planner; I wanted to be perceived as prepared, polished, and in control. Red glasses, red lipstick, professional dress. Agenda ready. No nonsense.

We all logged into Zoom. I greeted the group, asked for quick introductions, thanked them for their time, and promised I would honor it. Then I went right into the agenda.

One of the participants (who is now one of my closest friends) later told me her first impression: "*Wow. This chick is intense and serious.*"

We laugh about it now, because she knows the whole me:

- The polished professional *and*
- The life-of-the-party, Creative Free Spirit who will have the room laughing in 30 seconds flat.

Back then, though, all she saw was the mask I thought I had to wear.

I wasn't lying about who I was - I was just filtering. And that's where many leaders live: halfway between who they *are* and who they *think* they're supposed to be.

In a world of social media and filters, people are disillusioned and often desperate to find real and relatable role models. We've all felt it - the polished LinkedIn posts, the "everything's fine" smiles, the curated leadership image. But underneath it all, people are craving something different: leaders who are human, honest, and present.

Authenticity in leadership isn't about oversharing or being sloppy with boundaries. It's about alignment-who you *say* you are, how you *show up*, and what people actually *experience* from you. When those three things don't match, you get a leadership emergency: disconnect, disengagement, and disappearing trust.

And yes, that means you and I must be brave enough to show up as ourselves.

The Pandemic: A Strange Gift of Vulnerability

It's hard to imagine that the pandemic gave us any gifts, but it did. One of those gifts was a forced vulnerability.

For the first time in my lifetime, I watched leaders at every level-from CEOs to charge nurses to school principals-say aloud, "I don't know." There was no playbook, no "right" answer, no one person with all the information. The playing field of leadership was suddenly leveled.

Before this, it always felt like *somebody* knew what to do. During the pandemic, *everybody* was scrambling to figure out what to do next: how to communicate, how to cope, how to survive the day. It was the first time I can formally remember leaders saying, "We'll have to do the best we can with what we know right now."

Ironically, that collective uncertainty gave people permission to be more honest. We saw kids crawling into Zoom meetings, pets on laps, tears in the bathroom, and exhausted eyes behind the camera. Titles didn't matter as much. Humanity did.

Authenticity moved from "nice idea" to "required equipment."

My Reality: No Sabbatical, Just Survival

During the pandemic, there were generally two camps of people:

- Those who got an unexpected sabbatical-paid without having to work, taking long walks, catching up on books or TV.
- Those who hustled harder because if they didn't work, they didn't eat.

I lived in the second camp.

Most of my in-person classes and trainings were cancelled for at least six to eight weeks, and things didn't begin to resemble "normal" for a year or more. As a self-employed single mom, that meant immediate financial pressure plus the emotional load of making sure my kids were okay.

At the same time, my leadership work around burnout and resilience was suddenly *exactly* what people needed. I was learning Zoom on the fly, pivoting to virtual sessions, and unintentionally accelerating a speaking career I thought I'd lean into after 2027 when both kids were out of high school.

Those Zoom sessions became sacred space - people stepping away from clinical units, classroom chaos, or home offices to breathe, to reflect, and to feel less alone. We weren't just sharing content; we were sharing *capacity*.

And in the middle of that, I was also serving as chair of Workforce Development for my local Chamber of Commerce, leading a volunteer committee of busy, high-capacity professionals.

Cue: The Mask.

The Authenticity Gap: Where Trust Starts to Erode

Here's the tension: people want to work with professionals, not train wrecks. But they do *not* need perfection. In fact, constant perfection feels fake-and when things feel fake, people pull away.

That gap between your true self and your performed self is what I call the authenticity gap. The wider it gets, the more it: drains your energy, confuses your team, and erodes trust.

And often, that gap is driven by one sneaky culprit: Imposter Syndrome, The Inner Critic in a Power Suit.

Imposter Syndrome is that nagging voice in your head that says:

- *"You're not really qualified."*
- *"Any minute now, they'll figure you out."*
- *"You shouldn't be here. You're not enough."*

It shows up when you step into a new role, lead a higher-level group, or sit at a table where you feel outmatched. Instead of saying, "I'm learning along the way," we tell ourselves, "I'm faking it until I make it."

I felt this with almost every leadership promotion I ever had. The story in my head went something like: *"If I don't have all the answers immediately, I'm not worthy of the role."*

Let me let you in on a secret:

When you're hired into a new role, no one expects you to have all the answers. They expect you to:

- Bring a strong foundation
- Be willing to learn
- Build relationships
- Ask good questions

But instead of admitting what we don't know, many of us put on a mask. We get:

- Overly formal
- Aloof or disconnected
- Defensive or rigid

And that mask, meant to protect us, ends up pushing people away. What they experience as arrogance or coldness is often just fear.

The cost? Less trust. Less honesty. Less engagement.

Introducing the P.A.P. Framework

As I've taught educators and leaders across North Carolina, I developed a simple framework to help leaders stay aligned with authenticity while still maintaining professionalism and accountability. It's called the P.A.P. Framework, and it applies far beyond the clinical and classroom setting.

This framework reinforces these core truths:

- Partnership without clarity is confusion.
- Authenticity without accountability is chaos.
- Professionalism without authenticity is cold.

P.A.P. gives leaders a way to balance all three.

P: Partner for Success

Partnership means we don't lead *at* people; we lead *with* them. It requires curiosity, mutual respect, and the willingness to remove the mask long enough to say:

- *"Help me understand what you're seeing."*
- *"What do you think is the best next step?"*
- *"What support do you need from me?"*

When leaders partner with their teams, authenticity becomes *safe*-because it's shared.
When partnership is missing, people either hide or harden.

A: Authenticity

Authenticity is about alignment between who you say you are and how you show up.

It is:

- Honest without being reckless
- Transparent without oversharing
- Consistent across levels, positions, and power dynamics
- Courageous enough to show humanity
- Humble enough to admit what isn't known

Authenticity is also contagious. When a leader models it, teams reciprocate with honesty, engagement, and connection.

P: Professionalism

Professionalism isn't perfection.
It is responsibility.

It's saying:

- *"I'll own my part."*
- *"Here's what I learned."*
- *"Here's how I'll make it right."*

Professionalism protects authenticity from becoming sloppy and protects partnership from becoming permissive. It creates a culture where people can be human and still be expected to do excellent work.

And when you combine all three; Partnership, Authenticity, and Professionalism; you get the essential through-line:

Accountability: the thread that holds it all together.

Authenticity without accountability becomes excuses.
Professionalism without authenticity breeds resentment.
Partnership without accountability creates dependency.

But when all three operate together, you get Focused and Fearless Leadership:

"Focused leaders partner with their teams."
"Fearless leaders show up authentically."

Transformational leaders hold themselves (and others) accountable in healthy, consistent ways.

The P.A.P. Framework is not just a keynote tool. It is the practical scaffolding of authentic leadership.

Authenticity as a Leadership Superpower

Here's the truth: authenticity is not a liability. It's a leadership *superpower.*

When you show up as yourself flaws, quirks, and all - you:

- Build trust faster
- Create psychological safety
- Invite real conversations
- Model what courage looks like

Think about a time when you felt completely comfortable being yourself:

Authenticity doesn't mean dumping your entire life story on your team. It means:

- Owning your strengths *and* your growth edges
- Admitting when you don't know
- Sharing lessons you've learned the hard way
- Letting your personality come through in healthy ways

That's where influence deepens.

Finding Your People: Your Authentic Inner Circle

Part of leading authentically is refusing to do it alone.

Over the past 15 years, I've been blessed with an inner circle of people who keep me humble, call me higher, refuse to let me shrink, celebrate my wins, and tell me the truth, even when it stings.

My previous pastor, Scott Bolton, always says: "Show me your friends and I'll show you your future." I also often say: "Smart people surround themselves with smarter people."

Your inner circle doesn't have to be CEOs or millionaires. It *does* need to be people who:

- Are grounded in their own lives
- Are not intimidated by your growth
- Celebrate you instead of competing with you
- Will call you out when you're playing small or hiding behind a mask

You know you've found your people when:

- You talk more about life than gossip about people
- You share your struggles and your wins
- You dream together about what's next
- You can say, "I messed that up," and they respond with honesty *and* grace

In my world, there's a phrase my tribe loves to hear: "Well, I just *Melissa'd* it."

That means I went in intending to be polished and perfect… and instead, I showed up gloriously human.

A "Melissa'd It" Moment

Recently, I was contracted by my former employer to provide training for the organization. I hadn't been back in about 10 years, so walking into that space was emotional. I saw people who had shaped my career, and we hugged like long-lost family.

The new leader who hired me walked in with another woman. I hugged the leader: I knew her from our night-shift ER days, and I was so proud of where she'd risen.

Then I turned to the other woman, assuming she was another old colleague. I went in for a big, enthusiastic hug. She pulled back slightly, surprised, and said, "Wow, I wasn't expecting this."

High on reunion joy and not fully catching the awkwardness, I smiled and said, "Well, if you're here, you must be family - so bring it in!"

And I gave her the kind of big-breasted, full-body hug only a thick woman can give.

She was... overwhelmed. I heard someone whisper:

"Wow, Melissa hasn't changed a bit!"

The room laughed. I laughed. Then the leader cleared her throat and said: "*Melissa, I'd like to introduce you to our new Chief Nursing Officer*."

Yep. I *Melissa'd* it.

Was that my dream first impression? Absolutely not. Was it authentic? Absolutely yes.

I blushed and said something like: *"Well, at least now you know what you're getting. I love the people in this organization and only want to see it succeed."*

Could an HR specialist write a policy case study about what *not* to do? Probably. Would I change it? Honestly... probably not.

Because here's my belief:

- Professionalism matters.
- Boundaries matter.
- *Connection* also matters.

Somewhere along the way, in trying to sanitize work, we've stripped out a lot of humanity. I wonder how much unnecessary turnover happens because people never experience real connection with their leaders.

When Leaders Put on a Different Personality

Authenticity isn't just about being warm or fun. It's also about consistency.

I once worked with a colleague who, whenever she was "in charge," became a completely different person. Her tone shifted. Her body language changed. She went from friendly peer to rigid, bossy dictator.

One day, I made a mistake at work. I immediately notified her so we could address it. She responded sternly and said I'd be "written up." I told her I already knew the process and was literally writing the report as she spoke. I was already upset with myself, and her reaction amplified the distress.

Remember the **T.H.R.E.A.T.** model from earlier?

- **T: Tribe** Are the others involved for me or against me?
- **H: Hierarchy Does** this person hold power, authority, or influence over me?
- **R: Reliability Can** I trust the leader and the process?
- **E: Empowerment** Will I have a voice or meaningful influence in the outcome?
- **A: Anticipation** Can I predict what's coming?
- **T: Timing** How soon will this happen and when will it be over?

Her reaction triggered all of them. Respect and trust dropped.

Several weeks later, she made a much more serious mistake. This time? No write-up. No ownership. It was shrugged off.

The inconsistency and lack of authenticity in how she handled mistakes (mine vs. hers) finished off what little trust I had left. I started avoiding working with her. Eventually, I took a different role altogether.

When a leader:

- Acts one way "at your level" and another when they have authority
- Demands accountability from others, but dodges it themselves

...their credibility evaporates. And once that happens, people mentally quit long before they physically resign. When your most passionate person goes silent, beware.

Authenticity, Accountability, and Grace

When I lead authentically and I make a mistake:

- My team knows my heart.
- They've seen me own my missteps.
- They've watched me apologize and make it right.

That doesn't excuse my errors, but it frames them. Because they know I recognize my own humanity, they're more likely to offer grace. And because I value that grace, I try hard to extend it to others.

It's not a matter of *if* I'll "Melissa" another situation, but *when.* So, I keep making deposits into the Bank of Grace:

- Listening instead of reacting
- Owning my part without defensiveness
- Allowing others to be human too (I like to call them learning curves.)

I've never regretted extending grace, even when, in hindsight, the person "didn't deserve it." Because at the end of the day, I'm just another flawed human trying to do the next right thing. And that, in itself, is a form of authenticity.

This is where Focused and Fearless Leadership gets very real: not in the moments when you look perfect, but in the moments when you are brave enough to be human - and still lead.

CHAPTER 7: FOCUSED & FEARLESS REFLECTIONS

"Focused leaders notice their mask. Fearless leaders dare to set it down."

Where do you feel the strongest pressure to "perform" instead of just show up as yourself-at work, at home, in your community, or online? What does that mask look like for you?

"Focused leaders own their story. Fearless leaders share the parts that help others."

What lesson from your own life or leadership could build trust if you shared it appropriately with your team-but you've been hesitant to say out loud?

"Focused leaders align their actions. Fearless leaders align their image and impact."

Where is there a gap between who you say you are as a leader and how people actually experience you? What is one small change you can make this week to close that gap?

"Focused leaders choose their circle. Fearless leaders let that circle tell them the truth."

Who in your life has earned the right to tell you, "You're not being yourself" or "You're playing small here"? How can you invite more honest feedback from them?

____

____

"Focused leaders model grace. Fearless leaders receive it, too."

When you make a mistake, do you tend to hide it, over-explain it, or own it and move forward? How might leading with authenticity and grace-toward yourself and others-change the culture around you?

____

____

> ***"Focused leaders show up real.***
> ***Fearless leaders show up whole."***

CHAPTER 08

Focused & Fearless Teams, Hiring Beyond Warm Bodies

"Focused leaders hire wisely."
"Fearless leaders inspire commitment and engagement."

There's something deeply personal about building something from the ground up, especially when it's more than a project. When we began LaunchJoCo, it wasn't just a professional development program. It was a mission: a county-wide, collaborative effort to uplift small businesses and equip entrepreneurs.

I poured my heart into it:

- Reviewing curriculum
- Co-selecting the instructor
- Nurturing relationships across chambers, funders, and community partners
- Showing up for every cohort session like it was sacred

From the very beginning, LaunchJoCo became part of my DNA. I poured as much volunteer energy into it as I did my own business.

Then came an unexpected opportunity: a chance to take The Overton Experience to a national stage - more speaking, more impact, more reach.

It was the kind of opportunity I had dreamed about. And it meant stepping back from LaunchJoCo for an entire year.

If the program depended entirely on *me*, this was the moment it could have collapsed. That's a leadership emergency in slow motion.

Focused and Fearless Leadership demanded that I practice what I preach.

Long before that opportunity appeared, I had:

- Invited a colleague into the inner workings of the program
- Shared templates, timelines, and communication plans
- Debriefed with her after sessions
- Let her lead pieces while I watched from the side

She didn't just know the process; she understood the heartbeat of the program.

So, when I stepped away, LaunchJoCo didn't just survive - it evolved.

- Alumni thrived.
- New ideas were implemented.
- Our partners stayed engaged.
- I got to cheer from the sidelines while stepping into a new season of my own mission.

That's when it hit me: Leadership isn't proven by how much falls apart when you leave. It's proven by how much keeps growing after you do.

Building a focused and fearless team means intentionally surrounding yourself with people who can step up, step in, and sometimes even surpass you.

Hiring warm bodies is about protecting your comfort.
Hiring and developing strong people is about protecting the *mission*.

Many leaders fall into the trap of reacting quickly to fill open positions. The pressure is real as production must continue, customers must be served, staffing grids must be met, and the rest of the team is already stretched. A rapid hiring decision *feels* like relief.

But in leadership, what feels like relief can quietly become a leadership emergency.

Pausing to think strategically about who you hire-and how you hire-is far more advantageous for long-term success than simply filling the vacancy. A warm body can stand in the spot, clock the hours, and still drain the life out of your culture, your productivity, and your credibility as a leader.

Many leaders fall into the trap of reacting quickly to fill open positions. The pressure is on to keep the workflow running smoothly and all of the team members happy. A rapid hiring process may seem like the perfect solution, but pausing to develop a response plan is far more advantageous for long-term success.

Two reasons come to mind:

1. Many leaders/hiring managers believe they need help immediately, and anyone is better than no one - WRONG. Hiring the wrong person for the team can actually lead to increased turnover of all staff including the new hire.

   Over the years, I have asked countless teams the same question. Would you rather hire people to fill the position that may not be a good fit OR would you rather work short until you find the ideal candidate? Every single time, the answer has ALWAYS been the same - "I would rather work short" often followed with some sentiment along the line of "as long as I know my leader was working on the right fit so we can stabilize this team." Yes, your team gets tired and leans toward potential burnout, but at the same time there is something energy boosting about knowing that your leaders are looking for those who will fit in with the team.

   What makes it even better is when the leader recognizes the need to have someone on the selection team who will be working with the new hire! It takes a little coaching to prepare the front line worker to join the interview process, but the reward is a different perspective. I have seen times where having this approach has created a more successful hiring process.

2. Leaders/hiring managers think that they want someone who can do the job, but they don't want the new hire to potentially be better than themselves (wrong). As a leader, it is our responsibility to find highly qualified talent. If their potential is threatening to you as a leader, then you should be looking at your own limitations and developing your own actions to know more and become more.

   We have developed a disposable culture. Everything is expendable. We don't have to take care of anything (e.g.,

> our team members, equipment, vendors, relationships) because there's always more ahead. Today, I know and see that building a team that can sometimes outperform me is a GREAT thing. I am creating a legacy organization that would miss me when I am gone but still be able to carry on with what I worked so hard to create.

Keeping those two concepts in mind, it seems to be commonplace in a lot of organizations today to recruit and hire people as quickly as possible. Many times, employers have low inventory to select potential employees from, and employees can pick and choose to accept job offers as they feel.

I sit on a few different committees locally and across the region that focus on recruitment and retention of the local workforce. It's disheartening to hear some of the conversations going on in the room. Some employers are tolerating employees coming late to work for their production line jobs, and their solution is to give a 5% bonus every day that their employee comes to work on time. "What happens if they come to work early on Tuesday, Wednesday, and Thursday but not Monday and Friday? What is the penalty?" Their answer, I kid you not, was "Well, then they only get the bonus for three days. There are no penalties. We are just glad they came at all." Others are enticing employees with jobs by giving them money, benefits, and now subscriptions to streaming apps like Netflix.

There are multiple reasons post-pandemic for this low inventory, including early retirement of aging staff, the loss of women in the workforce because of changed priorities, decreased access to childcare, and a boom in entrepreneurship with the desire for many to find ways to work from home. This has all led to a tight labor market.

Organizations find themselves looking at their job descriptions, minimum requirements for hire and their actual hiring process. Trends are moving away from formal degrees and back to more of an "on the job training" approach as I have learned from service on committees exploring workforce development.

It can be tempting to just hire a warm body, meaning the first person who checks the boxes on the surface, but it's detrimental to the big picture. When improperly screened, businesses will have breaks in productivity, and eventually, when the fit is really wrong, we will see turnover among the staff.

If you are the leader who prefers to look at data over employee morale, then stop and look at the harsh cost of turnover. When calculating turnover, it is crucial to consider lost employee production, the overtime for colleagues to create the work, as well as the cost of HR to process the termination, recruit, and onboard new help. The Society for Human Resource Management (SHRM) determined that the minimal cost of turnover for a front-line employee is 33% of their annual salary, a mid-level manager is 150% of their salary, and a C-Suite executive is 400% of their salary (Tyler 2021). Can we really afford to just hire warm bodies? Although all turnover is not bad turnover, it is important to pause for a moment to look at the big picture.

Are you aware of the concept called "Forming, Storming, Norming, and Performing? " Massachusetts Institute of Technology (MIT) has outlined this concept (MindTools.com n.d.):

Forming is the process of hiring and onboarding new team members. Ideally, new hires should be interviewed by a peer review process, as each person on the peer team will be most likely looking at this potential hire through a different lens. For example, HR may be looking for compliance and qualifications. Management may be looking at qualifications and willingness to communicate well. The colleague is looking at qualifications but also whether or not the person will be a good fit for the work culture.

Once there are changes made to the team dynamics, storming begins to occur. The team will start to become challenging and sometimes disruptive as everyone begins to exert where they fit into the dynamic. It is important to know that storming is normal but should not be a continuous thing. Once storming begins to disrupt organizational operations, it is the responsibility of management to come in and norm the process.

Norming is the process of defining the roles of the team members and clarifying any role confusion. Norming allows the team to settle down and then focus on the work at hand, which is the performing portion.

Performing is the sign of true productivity that cannot occur until the relationships and roles are clarified, which closely follows John Maxwell's Five Levels of Leadership model.

The challenge is that with every turnover, this process begins again. Depending on the role that is turned over, the level of disruption can vary.

John Maxwell has a principle called the "Law of the Lid" (Maxwell 1998, 2). The law states that often people will not allow others with more potential than themselves to work on their teams. The potential is seen as a threat and thus cannot be tolerated.

Going back to *The Five Levels of Leadership*, Maxwell demonstrates the progression of leadership success throughout the book. Level 1 begins with establishing credibility based on your potential which leads to relationship development. To finish the thought progression, Level 5 is when leadership creates other great leaders who create great organizations (Maxwell 2013).

As a leader of any group of people, we should always identify those with potential to join our team. As a leader, we should also recognize and insist on the continued development of our team so that they can become successful leaders should turnover occur.

As leaders, our job is not just to fill roles. It is to identify potential, develop people, and build a team that can keep succeeding even when we're not in the room.

Keep Growing or Start Declining

About 20 years ago, I read something about a ready moment, and it became my mantra. Everyone experiences ready moments in life, where the conditions are ripe to make a shift to grow. When we miss those moments (often due to fear and lack of focus), we stop growing and planning, which leads to decline. The same is true for teams and organizations.

I don't know about you, but I don't plan on being finished until I slide into my funeral. There's too much awesomeness to experience and share.

Focused and fearless leaders:

- Hire for mission, not convenience.
- Develop people for succession, not dependence.
- Build teams that can sustain the work long after their season in the end.

Warm bodies can fill space. Aligned and committed teammates can change everything.

CHAPTER 8: FOCUSED & FEARLESS REFLECTIONS

"Focused leaders hire for fit. Fearless leaders develop for future."

How intentionally are you involving the right people (HR, leaders, peers) in your hiring and onboarding process? What's one change you could make to improve the quality of your hires?

____

____

"Focused leaders build systems. Fearless leaders build successors."

If you had to step away from your role for a year-by choice or by circumstance-what would fall apart? Who are you actively developing right now so that the mission can continue without you?

____

____

"Focused leaders track turnover. Fearless leaders study what's underneath it."

Looking at your recent turnover, how much of it is a symptom of warm-body hiring, unclear expectations, or lack of development? What is one focused action you can take this quarter to strengthen your team, not just staff your schedule?

____

____

"Focused leaders lift the lid. Fearless leaders invite talent that stretches them."

Do you feel threatened by people on your team who are highly capable-or even more skilled than you in certain areas? What is one way you could intentionally leverage and celebrate their strengths instead?

"Focused leaders protect the culture. Fearless leaders refuse to trade it for convenience."

Where are you most tempted right now to "just get a body in the role"? What would it cost your culture-and your best people-if you did?

"Focused leaders read the storm. Fearless leaders lead through it."

When your team enters the "storming" phase after a hire or departure, how do you respond-as a firefighter putting out drama or as a guide helping them reach norming and performing?

CHAPTER

09

Focused & Fearless Leadership Across Differences

"Focused leaders notice differences. Fearless leaders leverage them."

I have the distinct honor of stepping into a Board Chair role for a local, forward-thinking nonprofit. It was not something I anticipated. When the need arose suddenly, it came with weight, responsibility, and more than a little uncertainty. After a great deal of prayer and reflection, I said yes.

I have served this organization as a volunteer for six years and held other leadership roles along the way, but this role is different. It carries a deeper level of stewardship and influence, and I do not take that lightly.

One of my most important responsibilities as Board Chair is identifying my vice chair and recommending new board members as seats become available. To me, this may be the most consequential work I will do during my year of service. Boards do not simply govern organizations. They shape culture, direction, and long-term impact.

Early in this transition, I met with the CEO for a candid conversation about the organization's mission and vision. We talked honestly about who currently holds influence at the board table, whose voices are shaping decisions, and where gaps in representation exist. Together, we made an intentional commitment to diversify our leadership, not as a symbolic gesture, but as a strategic imperative.

It is often easier to build a leadership team that agrees quickly and moves an agenda forward without friction. Consensus feels efficient. But focused and fearless leadership requires more than efficiency. It requires discernment, courage, and a willingness to sit with discomfort.

As a focused and fearless leader, I want a board that reflects the community we serve from multiple lenses. I want voices that challenge assumptions, question long-held practices, and help us examine issues from angles we might otherwise overlook. Excellence is rarely achieved by surrounding ourselves with people who think exactly as we do.

I am particularly excited about the generational diversity within our leadership team. A past board chair brings the perspective of a Baby Boomer. I represent Generation X. My vice chair is a Millennial. That combination matters.

Not because we are checking boxes or chasing trends, but because lived experience shapes how we see risk, innovation, communication, and responsibility. Each generation carries its own values, blind spots, and strengths. When those perspectives are respected and leveraged, leadership becomes more balanced and resilient.

I want to be clear. These leaders were not chosen solely because they represent different generations or viewpoints. Their leadership skills, influence, and commitment to the mission are exceptional. Diversity without competence serves no one. But competence paired with difference creates momentum.

In the sections that follow, I want to offer a brief overview of generational differences and the role of unconscious bias. Not to label or divide, but to illuminate why leadership across differences makes us stronger. When we understand how our backgrounds shape our perspectives, we become better collaborators, better decision-makers, and ultimately better leaders.

Focused leaders pay attention to who is in the room. Fearless leaders ensure the room is better because of it.

In the workplace, we are not all the same and that's not a problem to fix. It's a reality to honor.

We bring different:

- Generations
- Cultures and regions
- Family stories
- Personalities
- Belief systems
- Life experiences

Some of those differences are obvious. Many are not. In earlier chapters, we explored personality styles and how they shape communication. Now we'll look at two more forces that can either fuel leadership emergencies or unlock leadership excellence:

1. Generational differences

2. Unconscious bias

When leaders ignore or minimize these dynamics, they create misunderstandings, disengagement, and division. When focused and fearless leaders recognize and value them, they create connection, creativity, and stronger teams.

Generational Differences: The Story Behind the Story

We were never designed to be identical or to share all the same views. If we did, we would never experience innovation, course correction, or change.

Growing up in the 80s, I was taught to "live and let live." If someone didn't share my perspective and they weren't causing harm, I was taught to treat them with respect. It wasn't my job to judge or punish them.

Somewhere in the 2000s, something shifted. Our culture began to lose the ability to agree to disagree. Disagreement started to feel like an attack instead of a difference. This has fueled chaos and divisiveness that shows up everywhere from social media to boardrooms to break rooms.

Pair that with a tight labor market, and we now see people quitting jobs instead of working through conflict. Many of these conflicts are not about competence or character; they're about different generations crashing into each other with different expectations and assumptions.

Today, there are currently an unprecedented number of generations in the workforce creating a highly diverse age demographic. Each is shaped by different world events, parenting styles, and cultural messages. Understanding those formative forces doesn't excuse bad behavior but it does explain a lot.

Let's look at the broad strokes.

The Veteran Generation (born ~1920 – 1940)

Veterans are the "chain-of-command" generation. They grew up in the shadow of the Great Depression and World War II. They:

- Respect for authority and hierarchy
- Are fiercely loyal to family, community, and employer
- Are frugal and practical
- Often stay with one organization for most of their working life

If they are still working with you, they have often been there a *long* time. They are not thrilled about change, especially rapid change, and they absolutely expect to be respected for their years of service.

They are few in number now, but mighty in presence. I believe they are part of the greatest generation we'll see in our lifetime. Their influence will continue to be felt as the molded a lot of the senior executives that now lead.

Baby Boomers (born ~1940 – 1960)

Boomers are the original activists; think civil rights and women's rights. They:

- Questioned authority in ways their parents never did
- Grew up during economic expansion
- Experienced Vietnam and Korea, vastly different from the World Wars
- Often moved into leadership and executive roles

Many Boomers retired early during or after the pandemic, frustrated by rapid change, technology gaps, or fatigue leaving both a manpower gap and a knowledge gap.

Boomers often hold the "why behind the what" of an organization. Simon Sinek reminds us that people don't buy *what* you do, they buy *why* you do it. Wise leaders will capture Boomer wisdom before it walks out the door for good.

Generation X: The "Keep It Real" Generation (born ~1960 – 1980)

Gen X was shaped by:

- Rising divorce rates and two working parents
- Being "Latch Key Kids" with the house key on a chain
- Watching the Challenger explosion live, then going back to class with no debrief
- Experiencing corporate restructuring and limited promotion options

Many Gen Xers were raised with Veteran-style values:

- Respect authority
- Work hard
- Go outside and play
- Don't expect life to be fair

They watched their parents' jobs become less stable and learned that sometimes, you have to move companies to move up. They also absorbed a powerful survival lesson: "Life goes on. So do you."

Millennials / Gen Y (born ~1980 – 2000)

Millennials were shaped by:

- Parents who were often Boomers - activists, volunteers, advocates
- A culture of service, cause-driven work, and "make a difference"
- Columbine and 9/11 - events that traumatized, but also united, communities
- The rise of debriefing, counseling, and emotional intelligence in schools
- Helicopter parenting - high involvement, constant monitoring
- A "you're special" and "you can be anything" message
- Participation trophies and continual feedback

This created a generation that is:

- Highly engaged and service-oriented
- Often confident and at times, perceived as *too* confident
- Used to frequent feedback and affirmation

When Millennials entered workplaces led by Xers and Boomers, major disconnects surfaced:

1. **Gen X and older:** Feedback usually meant something was *wrong*. If no one said anything, it meant, "You're fine. Keep going."

2. **Millennials (and later Gen Z):** Constant feedback meant, "You are seen, you matter, and you're on track." When the feedback *stopped*, they assumed, "I'm failing."

Now that Millennials are stepping into senior leadership roles, they are often the leaders most likely to give frequent feedback. This is healthy but can feel condescending or unnecessary to older generations who see it through a different lens.

When I teach this, you can almost *see* the light bulbs turn on in the room. Suddenly, people stop taking things so personally and start saying, *"Ohhh... that's why we keep missing each other."*

Gen Z – The "Coronials" (born ~2000 – 2010)

Gen Z has never known a world without:

- The Internet
- Cell phones
- Social media

They have access to everything; the inspiring, the disturbing, and the flat-out fake news. While older generations went to a library or talked to elders, Gen Z has an algorithm in their pocket. They would rather look it up than ask questions or risk looking vulnerable by asking.

For parents trying to raise kids with specific values, this creates tension: whatever perspective a child has, the Internet will offer someone who agrees with it. We can limit access but rarely eliminate it.

Add to this:

- Social media pressure to appear perfect
- The constant possibility of being recorded or going viral
- Less unstructured outdoor play
- More screen time and less face-to-face communication

And we get a generation that is:

- Highly connected digitally
- Often awkward interpersonally

- Raised by Gen X "keep it real" parents who told them, "Life is hard. Nothing is promised. Sometimes you do everything right and still lose."
- Deeply impacted by the pandemic
- Experiencing anxiety at levels some studies compare to psychiatric inpatients in the 1950s

In the workplace, Gen Z's anxiety often shows up as:

- Cockiness
- Anger
- Impatience for promotion
- A belief that online information equals real-world readiness

Many have limited work experience before their first "adult" job. They need:

- Clear boundaries
- Structured expectations
- Coaching on professional norms
- Opportunities to prove competence and earn autonomy

And for what it's worth: every generation has predicted that the next one would be "the end of civilization." Yet with time, maturity, and opportunity, each generation rises and contributes.

Generation Alpha (Born 2010 – Present)

Generation Alpha follows Generation Z, which is often described as a shorter generation span than the traditional twenty years. That compression isn't accidental. Generational boundaries have tightened:

- Because the pace of societal, technological, and cultural change has accelerated.

- Major global events now reshape behavior, values, and communication styles faster than they once did.
- Generations are being defined more by shared formative experiences than by a fixed number of years.

Although Generation Alpha is only beginning to enter the earliest stages of the workforce, it is already influencing it. They are not leaders yet, but they are active observers of leadership behavior right now.

This generation has been born into a world where crisis feels constant:

- Technology overload is everywhere.
- Global health emergencies are part of their baseline reality.
- School lockdown drills *(run, hide, fight)* have replaced the tornado drills that defined my early school memories.
- They see adults who are often distracted, overstimulated, reactive, and increasingly outspoken about their opinions.

As a result, Generation Alpha is developing an astute threat-detection system.

- They notice when actions don't align with stated values.
- They see inconsistency between words and behavior.
- They observe leaders and authority figures struggle with emotional regulation in real time.

Cross Generational Communication

Generation	Years	Key Influencing Events	Common Workplace Traits	Effective Leadership Strategies
Veterans 	**1928-1945**	Great Depression, WWII, post-war rebuilding	Loyal, disciplined, value hierarchy, strong work ethic	Honor experience, provide structure, communicate clearly
Baby Boomers 	**1946-1964**	Post-war prosperity, Civil Rights Movement, Vietnam War	Mission-driven, competitive, value recognition	Acknowledge contributions, invite mentorship, tie work to purpose
Generation X 	**1965-1980**	Economic recessions, latchkey childhoods, early tech, Challenger	Independent, pragmatic, adaptable	Offer flexibility, focus on outcomes, build trust
Millennials 	**1981-1996**	9/11, Great Recession, student debt, rapid tech growth	Collaborative, feedback-driven, purpose-oriented	Coach regularly, provide growth paths, encourage collaboration
Gen Z 	**1997-2012**	COVID-19, social justice movements, digital-native world	Authenticity-driven, mental-health aware, entrepreneurial	Create psychological safety, explain the why, build skills
Gen Alpha 	**2013-2025**	AI, remote learning, global disruption, digital immersion	Highly tech-fluent, visual learners, expect personalization	Model boundaries, teach critical thinking, emphasize human skills

If you remember the early chapter on leadership lessons learned as we grow up, this generation is absorbing those lessons in an environment with more visible dysfunction than organization. They are watching how easily adults become triggered and how those triggers escalate or de-escalate situations.

They are learning, quietly and constantly, what leadership looks like under pressure.

That reality matters.

As we move forward in an increasingly blended workforce, understanding generational differences is no longer optional. But this understanding is not about putting people into boxes. It is about recognizing the **formational stories** that shape how individuals listen, respond, collaborate, and lead.

When leaders understand those stories, they gain language.
They gain empathy.
They gain practical strategies to communicate more effectively across generations.

Focused & Fearless Leadership requires this awareness, because the leaders of tomorrow are already watching how we lead today.

The Red Food Story: A Simple but Powerful Example

When I was little, I refused to eat ANYTHING red: no ketchup, spaghetti sauce, or red Kool-Aid. My aunt once served me spaghetti, and I covered it with mustard and parmesan just to choke it down.

Finally, she asked, "Melissa, why on earth do you do that?"

I answered, very seriously, "Because if I eat red things, that means I love the devil."

"What?!"

No one had ever told me that. Most images I saw showed God/Jesus in white or blue and the devil in red. My child brain made the connection: red = devil. Devil = bad. So obviously, red food must be off-limits.

That's how bias works. It's often unexamined, illogical, and deeply influential until someone helps us surface it and question it.

Today, if you know me, you'd laugh - red lipstick, red glasses, red everything. Somewhere along the way, I challenged that bias and let it go.

But imagine if I hadn't. Imagine if I believed that anything red was evil. As a leader, it would be my responsibility to know that bias and ensure it never translated into my behavior especially in high-stakes situations.

Unconscious Bias: The Lens You Didn't Know You Were Wearing

Anytime we deal with human beings, we must talk about unconscious bias.

In earlier chapters, I mentioned how our culture drifted into "cancel culture"- a world where if we disagree, we are done with each other. That doesn't work in leadership, and it certainly doesn't build strong teams.

Unconscious bias is the way our brains automatically categorize people and situations to make sense of the world. That wiring is shaped by:

- Who raised us
- What we were taught directly and indirectly
- What we saw modeled
- Where we grew up (region, community, culture)
- What we experienced in childhood and adolescence

It can be a blessing or a curse.

I like to think of it like this: when we're learning from someone, we should "copy their good habits and refuse their bad ones." But as kids, we don't have that discernment yet. We absorb everything; fears, prejudices, assumptions, and all.

We don't just categorize by race, gender, or religion. We also categorize by:

- City vs. country
- Accent or dialect
- Education level
- Political language
- Job role or income
- Appearance and style

The problem isn't that we *have* biases. The problem is when we don't know we have them and we act from them as if they are facts.

Bias Under Pressure

We are most likely to act from unconscious bias when we are:

1. Multitasking

2. Tired

3. Stressed

4. In crisis

Remember the active shooter training story? I didn't want to take care of the loud, cursing victim. My instinct was, *"If he's yelling, he's probably okay. Let someone else handle him."* That was a moment of bias based on behavior and noise level. I had to consciously redirect my focus to ensure care was equitable.

If I were still working in the ER and a whole team came in wearing bright red jerseys and if I still believed red was "bad" I would need to be exquisitely aware of that bias. Professionalism demands that my personal lens never affects the quality of care they receive.

The same is true in leadership:

- If you unconsciously see a certain accent as "less intelligent," you may talk over people without noticing.
- If you see visible tattoos as "unprofessional," you may underestimate talent sitting in front of you.

If you assume younger employees are entitled, or older employees are inflexible, you may miss the very strength your team needs.

You don't owe anyone a public list of your biases. But you do owe your team enough self-awareness to keep your biases from causing harm.

UNCONSCIOUS BIAS MOVING FROM REACTION TO REFLECTION

1. **NAME IT:** Ask yourself: What stories did I absorb growing up about race, gender, money, work ethic, "good" people, "bad" people, city people, country people?

2. **EXAMINE IT:** Does this belief match what I now know to be true? Does it align with my current values?

3. **DECIDE WHAT TO KEEP & TO RELEASE:** Some beliefs will still feel grounded and aligned. Others will crumble under the weight of experience and truth.

4. **CREATE INTERNAL "GUARDRAILS':** Especially under stress, ask: Could any of my biases be influencing how I'm reading this person or situation?

5. **INVITE FEEDBACK:** Invite feedback. When someone bravely points out a potential bias, resist the urge to get defensive. Their perspective may be a gift.

Moving From Reaction to Reflection

Unconscious bias will not disappear. But we can:

1. **Name it.**
   Ask yourself: What stories did I absorb growing up about race, gender, money, work ethic, "good" people, "bad" people, city people, country people?

2. **Examine it.**
   Does this belief match what I now know to be true? Does it align with my current values?

3. **Decide what to keep and what to release.**
   Some beliefs will still feel grounded and aligned. Others will crumble under the weight of experience and truth.

4. **Create internal "guardrails."**
   Especially under stress, ask: Could any of my biases be influencing how I'm reading this person or situation?

5. **Invite feedback.**
   When someone bravely points out a potential bias, resist the urge to get defensive. Their perspective may be a gift.

> "***Focused and fearless leaders don't pretend to be unbiased. They commit to being self-aware, accountable, and willing to grow.***

CHAPTER 9: FOCUSED & FEARLESS REFLECTIONS

"Focused leaders examine their lenses. Fearless leaders adjust them."

When you honestly inventory your own biases about age, background, education, appearance, or region; what patterns do you notice? Which one no longer matches the leader you want to be?

___

___

"Focused leaders check their bias. Fearless leaders invite accountability."

How do you respond when someone hints at or directly calls out a possible bias in your words or decisions, or do you pause to reflect, ask questions, and learn?

___

___

"Focused leaders make room at the table. Fearless leaders make sure every voice is heard."

Are there people or perspectives on your team that are unintentionally marginalized or consistently overlooked? What is one concrete step you can take this month to elevate diverse voices in discussions, decisions, or development opportunities?

___

___

CHAPTER 10

Frontlines Hold the Answers

"Focused leaders listen. Fearless leaders act."

Here's a healthcare example that affects almost all of us at some point because we will either be hospitalized ourselves or love someone who is.

In 2004, the Institute for Healthcare Improvement launched the 100,000 Lives Campaign, promoting the use of Rapid Response Teams in hospitals. The idea was simple and radical:

Patients often show signs of deterioration for up to six hours before cardiac arrest. If someone could call for a second set of eyes early, many deaths could be prevented.

These teams weren't called just for full-blown emergencies. They were called when something felt *off*:

- A combative patient who might actually be oxygen deprived
- Subtle signs of sepsis that hadn't yet been recognized
- Low blood sugar changes in behavior
- TIAs or chest pain that could signal a major event coming

Hospitals could choose whether to participate or not. Many formed committees to "explore feasibility."

At my hospital, our ICU director, Rebecca, saw the value immediately. Instead of letting it get buried in months of meetings, she:

1. Went straight to the frontline responders: the ICU team who already responded to codes.
2. Asked, "Do you see a need for this?"
3. Heard a resounding, "Yes. We're already seeing patients too late."

4. Took their lived experience to administration and requested to launch quickly.

She wrote the policy and procedure, leaned into her team's wisdom, and moved.

That decision changed lives.

Kandice's Call

At the time, I was an educator working with nineteen brand-new graduate nurses. I introduced the Rapid Response concept on a Friday and brought them back together on Monday for discussion.

Before I could even get started, one of the shyest nurses, Kandice, raised her hand.

She said, *"I used it."*

She had come back from a day off to find a patient she previously cared for now in restraints, angry, and agitated. The family was exhausted and upset. Kandice knew this man as pleasant, fully alert, and oriented. Her gut screamed *something is wrong.*

She approached the nurse assigned to him and suggested calling the new Medical Response Team (MRT). The nurse bristled:

"Honey, I've been a nurse for over 20 years. I'm not calling anyone. I know how to do my job. I'm not going to let you, fresh out of school, tell me what to do."

Kandice stood her ground.

"Oh yes, we are. Anyone has the right to call the MRT for a second opinion. And if you have a problem with it, call Melissa Overton."

When she said that in front of the group, my heart stopped. I felt pride that she spoke up, protective "mama bear" energy, and fear that if this went badly, every new nurse would be scared to ever call again.

Kandice called anyway.

The team responded. They assessed the patient with fresh eyes and quickly realized he wasn't "being difficult," he was hypoxic. His agitation was his brain begging for oxygen.

They intervened. He was transferred to the ICU.

Kandice saved his life.

And here's the key leadership lesson:

She could only do that because someone *upstream*, Rebecca, had listened to the frontline, implemented a new process, and empowered staff at *every* level to use it.

Kandice also called again later that shift for another patient who needed help. Once you experience that kind of impact, you don't forget it.

Listening, Learning, and the Power of Data

The original goal was 100,000 lives saved. Within a year, the campaign had to be renamed the 5 Million Lives Campaign because early results were so powerful.

A decade later, I was asked to review our hospital's data. The Rapid Response process had reduced in-hospital cardiac arrests by about 50%.

Digging deeper, I found many of the remaining cases were patients who arrived already beyond saving (EMS couldn't call time of death before arrival), OR were too sick to save, even with aggressive interventions, but families weren't ready to stop.

In other words, most of the preventable emergencies had been prevented.

Not because someone in leadership dreamed up a brilliant idea alone, but because leadership listened to the people closest to the work, implemented a structure that honored their instincts, and backed them up when they spoke up.

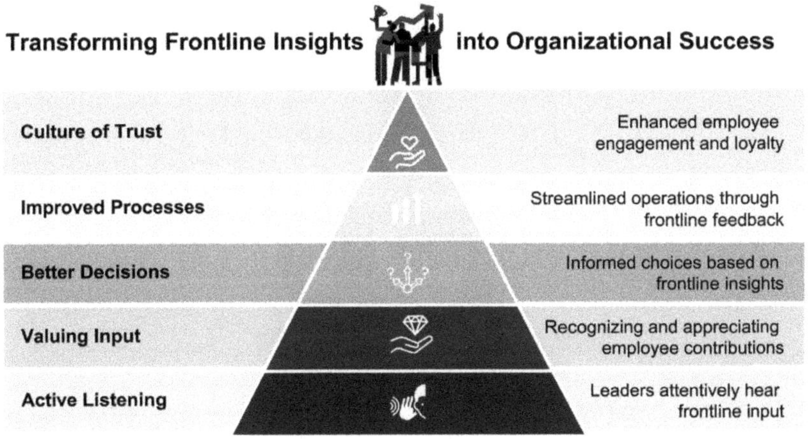

That's the opposite of a silenced team. That's a focused and fearless frontline.

How many times have you watched an organization try to fix a problem by forming a task force in a conference room without ever talking to the people who actually do the work?

Instead of walking down the hall, pulling a few frontline staff aside, and asking, "What are you seeing? What would actually help?" leaders schedule months of meetings, build complicated PowerPoints, and "reinvent the wheel" from a distance.

I am a firm believer that your first and best resource is your frontline.

- They know where the process actually breaks.
- They know which workarounds people quietly use.
- They know what's been tried before-and why it did or didn't work.

When we ignore them, we don't just miss solutions. We damage trust. We create leadership emergencies.

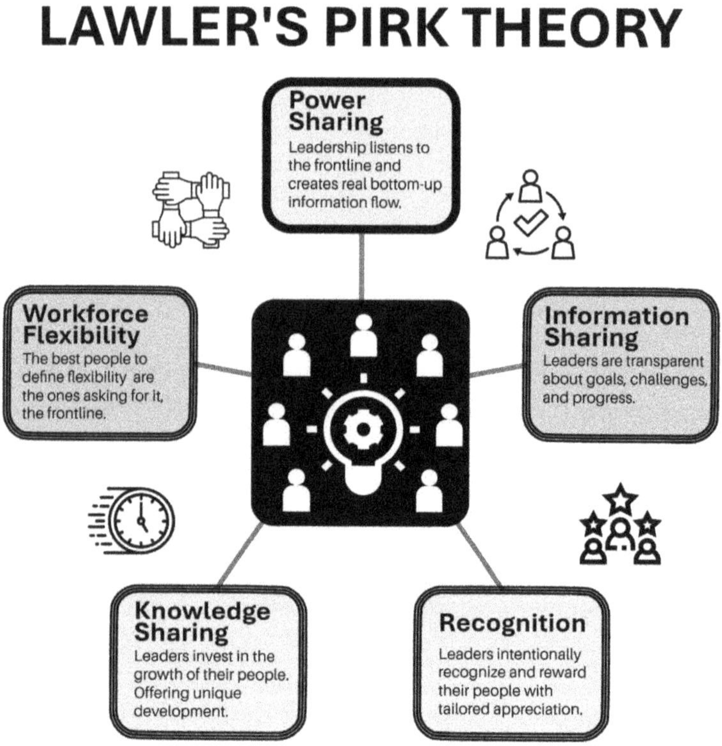

The PIRK Formula: The Secret Many Organizations Ignore

In the 1980s, Lawler's PIRK Theory was introduced in healthcare, and during my research to develop the Illuminated Training Next Level Leadership Program, I came across it. I vehemently believe that it is THE secret formula to organizational success and have taught this theory to all work sectors from banking to healthcare to manufacturing. Here is the premise - PIRK says great organizations hinge on four tenets (Tyler 2021):

- **P: Power Sharing**
  Leadership listens to the frontline and creates real bottom-up information flow. People closest to the work are invited to shape how the work is done.
- **I: Information Sharing**
  Leaders are transparent about goals, challenges, and progress. When people know what's really going on, they feel trusted, and act like owners, not just employees.
- **R: Recognition**
  Leaders intentionally recognize and reward their people, not only with money, but with tailored appreciation. They understand that recognition is not one-size-fits-all.
- **K: Knowledge Sharing**
  Leaders invest in the growth of their people. Yes, there's always a risk someone will take their new skills elsewhere. But more often, they stay, because most competitors don't offer that kind of development.

Years later, the Harvard Business Review and SHRM echoed the same themes, adding one more: workplace flexibility.

Flexibility looks quite different in a 24/7 operation than in a traditional office. But that's exactly the point: the best people to help define what flexibility *can* look like are the ones asking for it, the *frontline.*

Why "The Why Behind the What" Matters (Sinek, 2009)

When you introduce change, your team will almost always have an initial reaction: resistance. We are creatures of habit.

But here's the leadership lever many miss:

When you explain the *why behind the what,* people are far more willing to try, even if they think the idea is terrible.

They may still disagree. They may still believe it won't work. But if they understand:

- What you're trying to achieve
- Why this approach was chosen
- How you'll measure success (and adjust if needed)

...they are much more likely to give it a fair shot. And if it fails, they're more likely to say, "We tried. Here's what we learned," instead of "We told you so. Good luck next time."

Listening Beyond Healthcare

You may not work in a hospital, but the principles are universal.

Mid-pandemic, I was contracted by a bank to provide culture and communication consulting. When I first met with the CEO, I listened carefully to his request. He said, "Culture is very important to me. I heard you speak about teaching others to communicate better by first understanding each other more, so I want to see what you would recommend."

He challenged me to come to the bank as a secret shopper so I could experience the culture firsthand. I did exactly that. Afterward, we met again to discuss my assessment and recommendations. I still remember him saying, "I don't want a flash-in-the-pan experience. I want this done right."

As I created the proposed curriculum, I had a frank discussion with him about what his request would truly require. I wanted to ensure he understood that meaningful culture change takes more than teaching a class. That is when I introduced him to the PIRK Theory and explained why you have to do all of it for the work to stick. I had watched too many programs come in and "wow" a team, only to create little to no lasting change.

The magic is not in a single training moment. The magic is in listening to your team, leaning into their recommendations, and communicating clearly when certain ideas cannot be implemented, and why.

After implementing this curriculum, their staff engagement scores increased by 28 points in one quarter. As they continued the work we began together, they reduced turnover from 20% to 7% over two years.

If you would like to read the details, you can visit my website at https://www.melissaoverton.com. You will find it under the Illuminated Training tab, scroll down to the Corporate & Finance Case Study. And if you want to hear me get really excited, reach out and let's talk about how it all happened. It was an incredible experience, and to this day, that organization continues to thrive and shine.

And there is one more reason I will always remember that project.

It is the reason this book was written.

That CEO kept pushing me to write it. I resisted, because there are already so many leadership books in the world. But he kept saying, "Melissa, you do it differently. You teach it differently. A lot of people need to hear it your way."

He is also the one who wrote the foreword to this book.

He did not write it because he agreed with every idea easily or because the work was comfortable. He wrote it because he experienced everything I share in these pages firsthand. He lived it alongside his team, stayed committed when the work became challenging, and watched his organization not just improve, but shine.

That did not happen by accident.

It happened because he chose, day after day, to be a Focused and Fearless Leader. He chose to listen when it would have been easier to defend, to slow down when urgency tempted him to rush, and to lead by example when others were watching closely.

Focused and Fearless Leadership is not about perfection. It is about the daily decision to do the hard things. Leading by example is one of the hardest choices a leader can make, and it is also the one that creates the most lasting impact.

To be a Focused and Fearless Leader, I challenge you to make a **P.A.C.T.** to be:

P: Proactive **A:** Accountable **C:** Consistent **T:** Transparent

Your strategy to best achieve this is to **L.I.S.T.E.N.**

L: Look for patterns, not just complaints

I: Invite input consistently, not occasionally

S: Stay curious, not defensive

T: Thank your colleagues for speaking up

E: Explain what will happen next

N: Notify colleagues of actions taken

- L: Look for patterns, not just complaints
- I: Invite input consistently, not occasionally
- S: Stay curious, not defensive
- T: Thank your colleagues for speaking up
- E: Explain what will happen next
- N: Notify colleagues of actions taken

When you listen to your frontline, you:

1. Avoid reinventing the wheel.
   They already know what's broken and often have ideas for fixes.

2. Increase buy-in and ownership.
   When people are heard, they are far more likely to support and champion new processes, even hard ones.

3. Build respect and loyalty.
   Listening communicates, *"You matter. Your perspective counts. You are a valued part of this team."*

Listening does *not* mean you implement every suggestion. It means you create a culture where speaking up is expected, safe, and impactful.

- Silenced teams become resentful teams.
- Resentful teams become disengaged teams.
- Disengaged teams create leadership emergencies.

> ***Focused leaders break that cycle by listening. Fearless leaders complete the loop by acting on what they hear.***

CHAPTER 10: FOCUSED & FEARLESS REFLECTIONS

"Focused leaders walk the floor. Fearless leaders ask real questions."

What challenge are you facing right now that your frontline team likely understands better than you do? When was the last time you asked them directly for their perspective?

"Focused leaders invite input. Fearless leaders share ownership."

How could you involve frontline staff in shaping solutions-through focus groups, pilot teams, or peer-led problem-solving-rather than relying solely on task forces and leadership meetings?

"Focused leaders close the loop. Fearless leaders keep listening."

When you do try a new solution, how intentionally do you circle back to the people doing the work to ask, "Is this actually helping? What needs to be tweaked?"

"Focused leaders protect psychological safety. Fearless leaders defend those who speak up."

Think about your own "Kandice" stories. When someone newer or less experienced pushed back or raised a concern, how did you respond? Did your reaction make it more or less likely they, and others, would speak up next time?

"Focused leaders learn from what works. Fearless leaders scale it."

Where have frontline ideas already led to better outcomes in your organization? How can you capture those wins, celebrate them, and build systems that make listening to the frontline a *normal* part of how you lead, not just a one-time success story?

CHAPTER 11

Accountability in the Shadows - When Leaders Allow Less Than Average

---

"Focused leaders make space to listen. Fearless leaders act on what they hear."

In leadership, you are never an island. Your impact is always filtered through the people around you, especially the ones you quietly hope will change "on their own."

I once worked with a coworker I'll call "Bob". Bob had been with the organization longer than I had. He knew the routines, the politics, and exactly how much he could get away with. He was comfortable. Too comfortable.

As our roles began to overlap, so did our tension. I was the overachiever on a mission taking on new projects, improving systems, and saying yes to opportunities that would move the organization forward. That meant our shared manager expected more from both of us.

Bob did not appreciate this upgrade in expectations. He was used to a smaller workload, minimal collaboration, and being left alone. His frustration quickly turned into open resistance; snide remarks, stonewalling, and a clear message: *"I'm not changing, and you can't make me."*

I went to my manager devastated. I didn't want constant conflict, and I definitely didn't want to be the reason for it. She explained the stages of team development, how any change in roles or members brings turbulence, and promised to clarify expectations with the whole group.

That meeting helped on paper. Roles were defined. Goals were clarified. But in practice, Bob dug in even deeper. He became more abrasive, less cooperative, and more determined to do the bare minimum. For a while, nothing visible happened.

And that's where the leadership emergency started.

From my vantage point, my leader appeared silent. Maybe she was coaching him behind the scenes - that wasn't my business. But what *was* my business was the impact: Bob's behavior went unchecked long enough that it started to feel tolerated.

Eventually, leadership drew clear lines and consequences. Expectations were revisited, accountability tightened, and Bob was invited to either re-engage or move on. He chose to leave.

I didn't want him to be fired. I didn't enjoy the conflict. But once he was gone, the energy in the department shifted. It felt like a window had finally been opened in a stale room.

The lesson was clear: When leaders allow people to lurk in the shadows, the whole team pays the price.

The Hidden Cost of Tolerating Toxic Behavior

Toxic behavior is not always dramatic. Sometimes it looks like:

- Refusing to help a colleague who is clearly drowning
- Making cutting comments, then hiding behind "just kidding"
- Conveniently disappearing when the phone rings or the workload spikes
- Answering a simple request for support with sarcasm or hostility

When leaders don't address these patterns, they send powerful messages (whether they intend to or not):

1. "This is tolerated here." Your silence becomes permission.
2. High and mid-performers feel punished. They carry more weight while the "shadow dwellers" skate by.

3. Team cohesion erodes. People stop trusting you to protect the culture.

4. Turnover rises. Your best people leave long before your worst ones.

Accountability isn't about punishment. It's about *alignment* between values and behavior, expectations and action, words and reality. When you allow less than average to keep showing up, your culture becomes average at best, and dangerous at worst.

Why Communication Skills Matter More Than Ever

Since the pandemic, I've seen the demand for communication and conflict-resolution training explode. That's not a coincidence. A few things have collided:

1. Bandwidth for nonsense is at an all-time low. People are exhausted and less tolerant of dysfunction.
2. Anxiety has multiplied. Once you've lived through a world-stopping event, your nervous system stays on alert.
3. Digital generations are less practiced in face-to-face resolution. Hard conversations feel harder when you're used to hiding behind a screen.

All of this means:

Leaders can't afford to avoid conflict. You must learn to see it, name it, and navigate it.

That starts with understanding how conflict even gets started.

The (Hamster Wheel) Cycle of Conflict

Most conflict can be traced back to one (or more) of three root causes:

1. **Miscommunication**: What I meant is not what you heard.
2. **Unmet needs**: A request, expectation, or boundary wasn't honored.
3. **Different outcomes than expected**: Someone feels blindsided or disappointed.

When one of these happens, someone feels offended. They react. The other person reacts to the reaction. Suddenly, it's like two hamsters running on the same wheel; chasing each other in circles, going nowhere, and getting more exhausted by the second.

The only way out of the never-ending cycle? Somebody must choose to step off the "wheel" and ask the most powerful of questions:

- *"Wait? Did you really mean it the way I took it?"*

That pause is where accountability and grace can coexist.

The Power of Clarifying

I had a British colleague who was often misunderstood because of her accent and expressions.

One day, she had to track down a patient's allegedly "missing" belongings. After a lot of calls and detective work, she discovered the items were never lost. They had been picked up by a relative.

As the leader was leaving, my colleague sighed and said, "Wow, what a hassle."

The leader spun around, clearly upset: "What did you just say?"

My colleague repeated, "What a hassle," confused by the reaction. With her accent, though, the leader had initially heard something very different.

Instead of exploding, the leader checked her hearing before reacting. One clarifying question prevented an unnecessary conflict, hurt feelings, and likely a disciplinary process.

That's accountability, too:

- Accountability for what we *say*
- And accountability for how we *interpret* what we hear

Choosing to Respond Instead of React: The ABCDE Method

Dr. Albert Ellis created a cognitive behavioral therapy approach called the ABCDE Method (PositivePsychology.com 2025) that helps us slow down and choose our response. When a triggering event occurs, it suggests that we should systematically review our internal reaction before we choose to respond.

1. **A – Activating Event:** What actually happened? Depending on the timing of the event, we may not have interpreted what has triggered us from the right perspective. Taking a moment to reflect is going to be key especially if it has triggered an emotional response.

2. **B – Beliefs:** What am I telling myself about this event or this person's intent? Remember the cycle of conflict question? This is where it comes into play. "Did they really mean the way I took it?" My response is either going to escalate or de-escalate the situation.

3. **C – Consequences:** If I keep believing this story, how will I feel and act? How will this impact my future interaction

with this person? How will it potentially impact my reputation and image?

4. **D – Dispute:** Now after considering the potential consequences, it is important to reflect on two questions. Is there any other way to interpret this? Could I be missing something? This is a great stress test to ensure that emotion is removed and objectivity is in play.

5. **E – Energy/Effect:** Finally, what kind of energy do I want to bring into my response? How will my response, energize or effect the situation?

The Overton addition:

6. **FG – Find Grace:** With the current communication climate, where everyone still seems to be overloaded and the threshold to tolerate nonsense is lower than ever, take a moment to pause and give one last benefit of doubt which is what I call "find grace". I often pause and try to reflect on where this potential conflict and aggression is coming from.

Am I interacting with someone who is new to leadership and professional communication? Is something going on in their lives right now that is impacting their behavior?

This pause to Find Grace isn't a pass for bad behavior. Healthy communication and boundaries are still expected, but is there a reason that I should filter my response differently because of the circumstances that I find? This is so important in today's world where so many cultures, belief systems, work ethics are intermingling and communication comes in so many different forms: chat, SMS, email, voicemail, DM, Snap, tweet, and of course face to face.

As a Focused and Fearless Leader, I am constantly re-examining my thoughts and habits as a communicator. I am continuingly reviewing my own behaviors, as I teach best practice to others. Like any other human, there are days when I fall short. The filter falls off and something is said in the wrong way. I am triggered because in the moment, I was overloaded, and this one last thing was the last straw. When that occurs, I must go back to my own teachings and do what it takes to make it right. We must Find Grace in these moments, because some days we must also ask for someone else to Find Grace for our missteps.

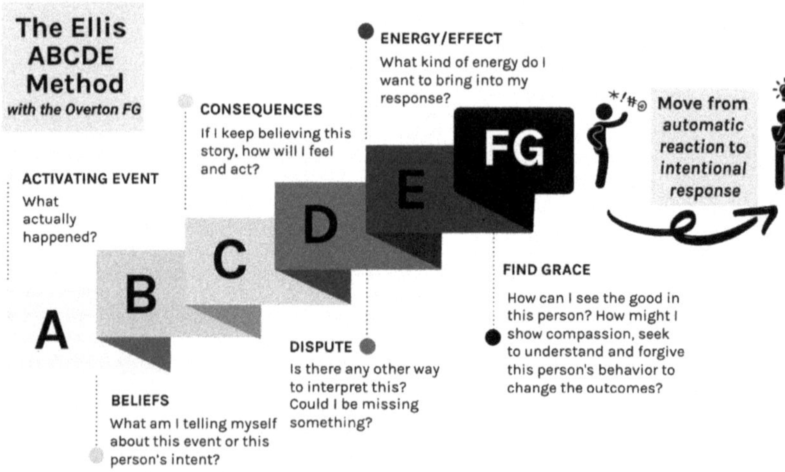

This framework forces us to move from *automatic reaction* to *intentional response, which is why I a*dded FG to this framework.

How many leadership emergencies could be prevented if we slowed down long enough to ask, "What else could this mean?"

Grace Without Excusing Harm: Leah and the Grandson

Accountability doesn't mean we never extend grace. It means we extend grace *without* abandoning safety or truth.

I once watched a nurse manager, Leah, do this brilliantly.

We were on the hospital's fourth floor when a man stepped off the elevator - intoxicated, distraught, and shouting,

"You're not going to take my grandma off the ventilator! You're not going to kill her!"

He charged us. Leah approached to try to calm him, and he swung at her. She dodged with a move that would make an action-movie director proud and firmly said,

"Whoa, brother. I grew up in the projects. I will take you down."

In that moment, she was in full contender mode - rightly so! Safety came first.

As his family rushed out of the ICU waiting room, they helped us piece together the story: They had called him to come see his grandmother as she was being taken off the ventilator *because she was doing so well*. He *misheard* and thought she was being removed from life support because she was dying. Fueled by alcohol, fear, and grief, he arrived ready to fight what he thought was a death sentence.

Once Leah understood, she shifted gears. She talked calmly with him, explained that his grandmother was improving, and helped him process the shock and relief. By the end, he hugged her, apologized, and agreed that he was in no shape to visit that day.

In under ten minutes, she had:

- Contended for safety
- Clarified the misunderstanding
- Extended grace
- Protected the team and the family

She held him accountable for his behavior *and* treated him like a human in pain. Her team saw it all and their respect for her skyrocketed.

How to Have the Hard Conversation

Not every conflict needs intervention. But when something is harming trust, performance, or safety, leaders must stop letting it lurk in the shadows.

Here's a Focused & Fearless framework to **C.L.E.A.R.** the obstacles:

C- Calm the space

Remove emotion. Choose a private place.

L- Listen first

Ask them to explain what happened- without interruption.

E- Echo understanding

Mirror and paraphrase what you heard to confirm clarity.

A- Assert your perspective

Use "I feel/I observed/I need" statements – no blame.

R- Resolve forward

Focus on the solution, discuss how to handle it in future and thank them for communication. "I know this wasn't easy. I appreciate you talking it through."

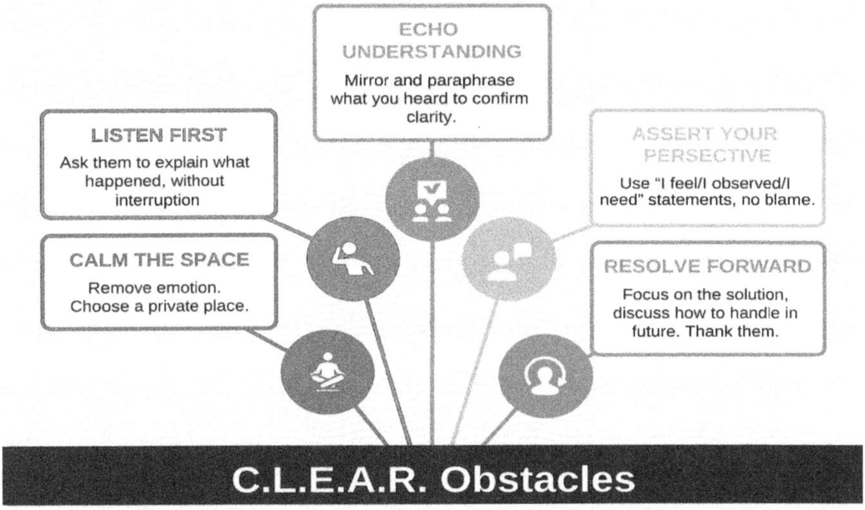

This process doesn't guarantee agreement, but it does guarantee clarity. And clarity is where accountability lives.

When Leaders Should Step In and When Peers Should

On the ER night shift, our team developed a rhythm: if we all hustled together, we could catch up and grab a brief breather between waves of patients. We covered for each other without keeping score.

Then a new colleague joined us. Every time work spiked, she suddenly had a headache, needed to chart, or disappeared. We tried gentle conversation. Nothing changed.

So, we made a conscious choice:

- We would still help when a patient's safety was at stake.
- But when she was overwhelmed *because* she hadn't been helping, we stopped rescuing her.

It didn't take long for her to understand that the team's support was reciprocal, not automatic. She adjusted her behavior and became a true partner.

Accountability isn't always top-down. Sometimes it's the culture saying, "We work together here. Hiding in the shadows isn't part of the deal."

Leaders shouldn't rush to referee every disagreement. Often, it's healthier and more empowering for peers to address issues directly.

In peer-to-peer conflict, a wise leader will:

1. Ask "Have you talked to them about this yet?"
2. Offer coaching on how to approach the conversation
3. Invite both parties to meet *together* if leadership involvement is truly needed

However, when behavior crosses into toxicity, e.g. chronic disrespect, sabotage, bullying, and/or safety risks, leaders must step in sooner rather than later.

Peer pressure can also be a powerful tool when used well.

Bringing People Out of the Shadows to Stop Toxicity

At its core, this chapter is about refusing to normalize less than average in ourselves, in our teams, and in our culture.

- Listening without acting creates resentment.
- Acting without listening creates rebellion.
- Focused & Fearless leaders listen + act and act + listen.

Your Role:

Your Role:

1) Make space to hear what's really going on.

2) Shine a light where behaviors don't match values.

3) Hold people, including yourself, accountable with both courage and compassion.

That's how you prevent leadership emergencies from festering in the dark corners of your organization.

CHAPTER 11: FOCUSED & FEARLESS REFLECTIONS

"Focused leaders see the impact. Fearless leaders address the source."

Where in your team or organization have you allowed a "Bob" to linger-someone whose behavior you know is misaligned, but you've avoided addressing directly? What has that tolerance cost you and your team?

____

____

"Focused leaders pause to interpret. Fearless leaders clarify before they conclude."

Think of a recent conflict or tense moment. How might using the ABCDE method or simply asking, "Did you mean it the way I took it?" have changed your response?

____

____

"Focused leaders shine light on shadows. Fearless leaders refuse to live with them."

What one step can you take in the next 30 days to reduce "shadow behavior" on your team-through clearer expectations, stronger follow-through, or healthier peer accountability?

____

____

"Focused leaders notice toxic patterns. Fearless leaders name them."

Which toxic behaviors (subtle or loud) are most common in your environment-sarcasm, avoidance, passive resistance, refusal to help, or something else? What conversation have you been avoiding about them?

____

____

"Focused leaders protect safety. Fearless leaders still offer grace."

Where do you need to contend firmly for safety, standards, or values and where do you need to intentionally layer in more grace, context, or curiosity?

____

____

"Focused leaders invite hard conversations. Fearless leaders stay in them."

What is one critical conversation you know you need to have this week with a peer, direct report, or leader? When will you have it, and what is one sentence you can use to open it with courage and care?

____

____

CHAPTER 12

Succession Gaps, When Leaders Don't Plan for Who's Next

"Focused leaders build capacity. Fearless leaders build backups."

Remember Maxwell's Law of the Lid (Maxwell 1998, 2)? Your leadership ability sets the limit on your organization's potential. If you stop growing, so does everything you touch. But there's another part we don't like to talk about:

- You are replaceable (and that's not an insult).
- You should be.

Early in my ER nursing career, I heard someone brag, "Leadership could never get rid of me. I'm too valuable to this place."

Before I could even roll my eyes, Dr. Murphy, the ER physician on duty, jumped in:

"Don't think for a minute that anyone is irreplaceable. People might adore you and respect you, but when you're gone, they'll miss you for a week, maybe a month if you held a big role. In a year, your name comes up in passing. A few years later, it's like you never existed.

Most organizations are machines. They will use you, replace you, and move on. It doesn't mean they don't appreciate you. Just don't confuse appreciation with immortality."

I remember thinking, *"Oh yeah? I'll leave such a mark they'll never recover when I'm gone."*

Cue the 23-year-old ER nurse, ten feet tall and bulletproof.

Spoiler alert: I don't work there anymore. And guess what? The ER still runs. Patients are still treated. New leaders have stepped up. Murphy was right; pretty much no one in staffing is even there anymore to remember me.

Here's what I eventually learned from that lesson:

1. You *will* be replaced. Maybe through promotion, retirement, relocation, illness, or a surprise life change.
2. If you care about impact, you must care about succession. That means identifying, preparing, and equipping those who will lead after you.

Leadership is not a destination; it's a relay. The question isn't *"How long can I hold the baton?"* but *"How well can I pass it?"*

When Vision Outran Succession

When I relocated to a new area, I joined a local women's group-business professionals united around fundraising and supporting women pursuing education and a better future.

A few years in, I was asked to take on a leadership role. Not because I was the obvious choice... but because someone else didn't want their name on it yet. I was the placeholder.

I laughed to myself. After years of building programs, leading hospital initiatives, and developing leaders across industries, I was still underestimated.

Here's a hard truth: It doesn't matter what you know until they know you. It really *is* about who you know and how well they know what you can do.

I accepted the "placeholder" title, and within a year the originally intended leader retired. Suddenly, the role was mine. Someone even called to "check" if I had what it took. I nearly choked from laughing.

Still, when I shared my vision, I was told:

"That won't work." That kind of doubt is rocket fuel for me.

So, I created a women's professional development conference. It aligned with my heart, my work, and my calling. The first year was a success.

The second year, with a new team alongside me, we doubled attendance from 50 to 100 (technically 99, but I'm claiming my 100). I gave the team credit publicly, and I meant it. But I also knew the truth:

- The attendees were largely my personal network.
- The vendors were my contacts.
- The model lived mostly in my head, so I worked hard to get the knowledge transferred and even left recommended timelines to plan the entire process.

I had *launched* something powerful, but it wasn't fully transferring back to the organization where I volunteered my time to do this.

By year three, I stepped back. I was tired, focused on growing my business, and I honestly believed the event would soar without me. I had proven what was possible. I thought the blueprint was clear enough.

It wasn't.

The event technically happened; but it shrank in energy, reach, and impact. At first, I was frustrated. I hadn't just walked away; I prepared them for it.

I built out the framework and even advised from the sidelines for this next event. It wasn't in my head. It wasn't vague. It wasn't unfinished. It was the exact blueprint for how to run a successful event.

But the new leadership team didn't embrace it.

Not because it was unclear. Not because it wasn't available. But because I was "just" a volunteer, and the plan wasn't valued.

The event didn't fail. It simply *shrunk*: less energy, less reach, less passion, and much less impact.

And the truth hit me: Succession plans don't work unless organizations CULTIVATE a culture that honors and implements them.

You can build the plane.
You can fuel the tank.
You can outline the flight path.

But if the next pilot refuses to get in the cockpit?

The plane doesn't fly.

Eventually, I joined another group who picked up a similar idea. This time, it became what I had always hoped for: a thriving, sustainable event with passionate team who shared ownership and a structure that didn't rely on any *one* person, not even me.

Now I work *with* them, not *above* them. And yes, some of them have absolutely surpassed me in organizing, scaling, and expanding the program.

That's not a threat; that's evidence of success.

Legacy Requires Legs

John Maxwell often says: "If you want to create a legacy, you have to give it legs."

If everything you've built collapses or shrinks the moment you step away, you haven't created a legacy, you've created a dependency.

Focused & Fearless leaders:

- **Name reality:** "I will not be in this role forever."
- **Spot potential:** They actively scan for people who could carry the work forward.
- **Share the blueprint:** Not just tasks, but *why* things are done the way they are.
- **Transfer relationships:** They introduce successors to stakeholders, vendors, partners, and decision-makers.
- **Practice letting go**: They step back in stages before they step out completely.

Succession planning is not morbid. It's responsible. It's generous. It's strategic prevention of a leadership emergency.

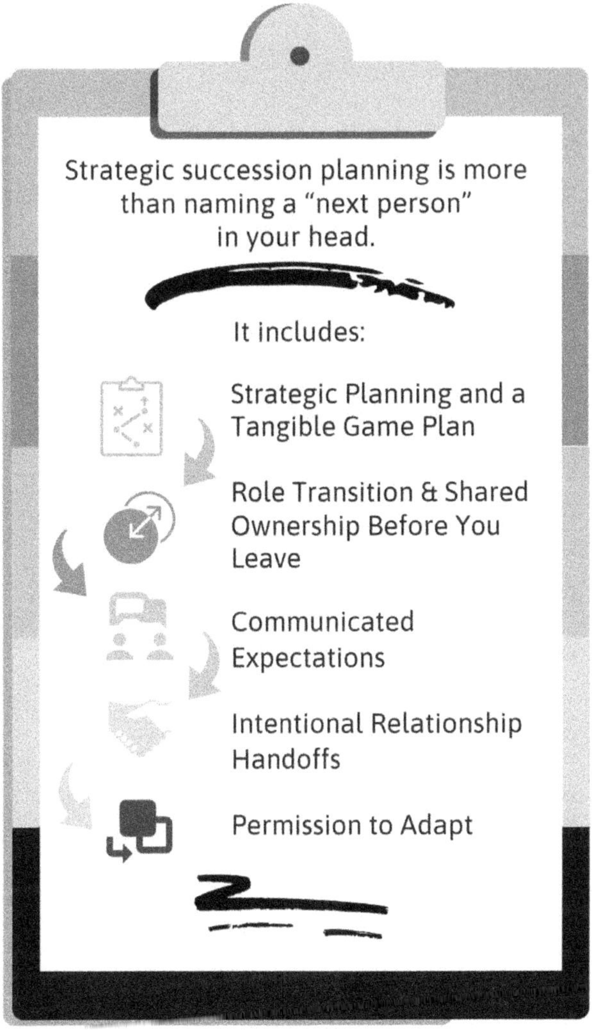
Strategic succession planning is more than naming a "next person" in your head.
It includes:
Strategic Planning and a Tangible Game Plan
Role Transition & Shared Ownership Before You Leave
Communicated Expectations
Intentional Relationship Handoffs
Permission to Adapt

What Succession *Actually* Looks Like

Strategic succession planning is more than naming a "next person" in your head. It includes:

1. **Strategic Planning and a Tangible Game Plan**
   - Timelines, checklists, key contacts, budgets, communication templates
   - "If I won the lottery tomorrow, could someone run this with what's written down?"
2. **Role Transition/Shared Ownership Before You Leave**
   - Invite emerging leaders into planning meetings, debriefs, and decision points
   - Let them run parts of the process while you're still there to coach
3. **Communicated Expectations**
   - Talk openly with your team: "Here's what I see for this program three years from now. Here's how I see you in that picture."
   - Normalize the idea that leadership will change hands because it will.
4. **Intentional Relationship Handoffs**
   - Bring your successor into conversations with sponsors, partners, and key allies
   - Say out loud, in front of others: "I trust them. They're leading this next phase."
5. **Permission to Adapt**
   - A good succession plan doesn't freeze your idea in time
   - It gives future leaders a framework *and* the freedom to adjust for new seasons

If your legacy depends on people doing it *exactly* your way, your legacy can quickly become obsolete.

When Leaders Don't Succession Plan

When leaders don't strategically succession plan, a few predictable emergencies show up:

- **Program Blackouts**: Amazing initiatives quietly die when a key leader moves, burns out, or shifts roles.
- **Panic Promotions:** People are thrown into leadership out of urgency, not readiness.
- **Knowledge Loss:** Institutional memory walks out the door every time a seasoned leader retires or resigns.
- **Resentment and Confusion:** Teams feel blindsided when no one knows who's in charge or what happens next.

These are not random crises. They are preventable leadership emergencies.

You don't control when every transition happens. But you *do* control how prepared your team is for when, *not if*, it comes.

CHAPTER 12: FOCUSED & FEARLESS REFLECTIONS

"Focused leaders think beyond today. Fearless leaders prepare for the day they're gone."

In the roles where you currently lead or influence, were you given a clear blueprint or "recipe for success" from the person before you? If yes, how did it help you? If not, what did it cost you?

____

____

"Focused leaders tidy their own path. Fearless leaders leave a map for others."

Where in your life (work, community, volunteer roles) are you currently building something without a written, shareable plan? What is one step you can take to start capturing that blueprint for the next person?

____

____

"Focused leaders protect what works. Fearless leaders improve it for who's next."

If you *do* have a succession plan or process, is it static or are you actively updating and improving it based on lessons learned? What's one part that needs to be clarified, simplified, or expanded?

____

____

"Focused leaders hold the baton well. Fearless leaders practice passing it."

Who are one or two people you could begin developing now to carry your work forward? How can you intentionally invite them into planning, decision-making, or relationship-building over the next 6–12 months?

____

____

"Focused leaders lead for this season. Fearless leaders lead for the seasons after them."

If you are *not* the formal leader, how can you share the importance of succession planning with those who are, without criticizing and alienating, but by casting a vision for sustainability, impact, and legacy?

____

____

Leading Focused. Living Fearless. Preventing the Crisis Before It Starts.

If you've made it to this point, you already know the truth I revealed in the very first pages:

Most leadership emergencies don't happen out of nowhere. They happen because we didn't mitigate the threat before it became a crisis.

Throughout this book, we have taken a focused and fearless tour through the most common leadership failures *and the proactive practices that prevent them.* From personal mastery to team dynamics to organizational culture, each chapter has been a reminder that leaders rarely fail from a single catastrophic moment. We fail in the moments we ignore, avoid, or underestimate.

Let's revisit the core patterns that cause leadership emergencies and the antidotes you now hold in your hands:

Core Patterns That Cause Leadership Emergencies

#1 **Self-awareness as your internal compass.**
Leadership emergencies often begin when we stop noticing ourselves. Focused leaders monitor their wiring, patterns, and reactions. Fearless leaders disrupt unhealthy ones before they spill out into the team.

#2 **Vulnerability and authenticity as stabilize.**
Influence grows when leaders drop the mask. Your team doesn't need perfection. They need truth, humanity, and consistency. Authenticity is a superpower. Use it!

#3 **Strategic hiring: never a "warm body."**
Teams break when leaders hire out of panic. Focused leaders hire wisely. Fearless leaders demand commitment, not just presence. The cost of a poor fit is far higher than the cost of waiting for the right one.

#4 **Valuing differences: generational, cognitive, cultural, experiential.**
Teams thrive when leaders understand that diversity isn't a buzzword; it's a performance multiplier. When you notice and leverage differences, you unlock creativity, resilience, and innovation.

#5 **Listening to the frontlines: where the truth always lives.**
Silenced teams create emergencies. The answers are almost always with the people closest to the work. Focused leaders listen. Fearless leaders act.

#6 **Eliminating the shadows: addressing conflict, communication, and accountability.**
If the environment is dark, toxicity thrives. Leaders must put so much light in the room that no "Bobs" or "Bobbies" can hide. Empowered teams communicate, resolve conflicts, and elevate each other.

#7 **Succession planning: ensuring continuity, not chaos.**
Great leaders don't just leave a legacy; they leave a plan. A blueprint. A backup. A culture where continuity is expected, embraced, and actively maintained.

The Hard Truth (and the Beautiful One)

Nothing in this book is "new." And that's the point.

Leadership isn't a mystery. It isn't a secret code. It isn't a trendy system.

It is a series of timeless principles that work ***when we apply them.*** You now have the frameworks, the psychology, the stories, and the tools. And as promised, you also have practical application embedded into every chapter through your Focused & Fearless Reflections.

The real transformation starts now.

Not when you close the book.
Not when you attend a retreat.
Not when you feel ready.

Now.

Leadership isn't what you know.
It's what you practice.

FOCUSED & FEARLESS REFLECTIONS & YOUR NEXT RIGHT STEPS

Use these final questions to operationalize everything you've learned.

What are the first two takeaways you will act on immediately?

- Look back through each chapter. Review your answers.
- Where can you begin today, not someday, to shift your leadership practice?

Who else needs this book?

Leadership isn't positional. It's relational.
Share these tools with:

- A rising leader
- A teen or young adult
- A colleague in crisis
- A burned-out team member
- A volunteer stepping into more influence

If they learn it earlier than we did, they will prevent the emergencies we had to live through.

Do you want to go further and deeper?

If your team, organization, or leadership group wants to:

- Build a culture of resilience
- Prevent leadership emergencies
- Strengthen communication and accountability
- Develop emerging leaders
- Create succession plans that truly work

...I would love to work with you. Together, we can design a focused and fearless strategy that elevates your people and your impact.

Your Final Charge

You now *know* what I know. You've seen behind "the curtain". You've learned the patterns that create crises and the practices that prevent them.

The question now is simple: *What will you do with it?* Because when you commit to leading focused and fearless... your team rises, your culture stabilizes, and your impact multiplies.

Let's go prevent some leadership emergencies...on purpose. Together.

Jeremiah, David. 2018. Overcomer: 8 Ways to Live a Life of Unstoppable Strength, Unmovable Faith, and Unbelievable Power. Nashville, Tennessee: W Publishing Group, an imprint of Thomas Nelson, Inc.

Kossek, Ellen Ernst, Patricia Gettings, and Kaumudi Misra. "The Future of Flexibility at Work." *Harvard Business Review*, September 28, 2021. https://hbr.org/2021/09/the-future-of-flexibility-at-work.

Maxwell, John C. 1998. *The 21 Irrefutable Laws of Leadership: Follow Them and People Will Follow You*. Nashville, TN: Thomas Nelson Publishers.

Maxwell, John C. *The 5 Levels of Leadership: Proven Steps to Maximize Your Potential.* New York: Center Street, 2013.

MindTools.com. n.d. "Forming, Storming, Norming, and Performing: Understanding the Stages of Team Formation." MindTools. https://www.mindtools.com/abyj5fi/forming-storming-norming-and-performing.

Porges, Stephen W. *The Polyvagal Theory: Neurophysiological Foundations of Emotions, Attachment, Communication, and Self-Regulation.* W. W. Norton & Company, 2011.

PositivePsychology.com. 2025. "What is Albert Ellis' ABC Model in CBT Theory? (Incl. PDF)." PositivePsychology.com, May 12, 2025. https://positivepsychology.com/albert-ellis-abc-model-rebt-cbt/.

Scott, Kim. *Radical Candor: Be a Kick-Ass Boss Without Losing Your Humanity*. New York: St. Martin's Press, 2017.

Simon Sinek. *Start with why: How great leaders inspire everyone to take action*. Portfolio, 2009.

Stanier, Michael Bungay. *The Coaching Habit: Say Less, Ask More & Change the Way You Lead Forever*. Box of Crayons Press, 2016.

Thomas, Kenneth W., and Ralph H. Kilmann. *Thomas-Kilmann Conflict Mode Instrument*. Tuxedo, NY: Xicom, Inc., 1974.

Tyler, Kathryn. "How to Ride the Great Resignation Wave." SHRM, June 2, 2021. https://www.shrm.org/topics-tools/news/hr-magazine/how-to-ride-great-resignation-wave.

Wachter RM, Pronovost PJ. The 100,000 Lives Campaign: A scientific and policy review. Jt Comm J Qual Patient Saf. 2006 Nov;32(11):621-7. doi: 10.1016/s1553-7250(06)32080-6. PMID: 17120921.

This book was born from decades of standing in the tension between chaos and calm -first at the bedside, then in the boardroom, and always with people at the heart of every decision. I've lived the reality that leadership is often less about having all the answers and more about showing up when it counts. Thank you to those who have walked with me, pushed me, challenged me, and trusted me through it all.

To my family (Mom, Burt , and Branden): your unconditional love is the root system that grounds everything I do. To my amazing children, Thomas and Lanie -you are my heartbeat. Thank you for giving me space to dream and room to lead. I couldn't do this without your grace, laughter, and a few truth bombs.

To my tribe of mentors, friends, colleagues, and clients, thank you for believing in me, sometimes more than I believed in myself. You helped me see that stories, scars, and stress-tested leadership moments are not weaknesses but wisdom worth sharing. A special thanks to Heidi Stieber and Earl Worley, who were relentless in their efforts to get me to see this book and its potential. Heidi, without you, this would have never hit the finish line. I love you!

A special thank you to David Rendall, author of "The Freak Factor". Thank you for the amazing advice to either: write the book in a series of blogs or choose to lock yourself away, write until your eyeballs bleed, and your fingers cramp up. As an ER nurse, I naturally chose option 2. Your selfless wisdom and guidance gave me the courage to get it done. You are a rockstar!

To every nurse, educator, chamber member, business leader, and student I've ever trained, coached, or shared space with-you're why I do this work. Your courage, vulnerability, and com-mitment to growth made this book real. You've shown me time and time again that we don't need perfect leaders-we need pre-sent ones.

To my MedicalTraining.me, LaunchJoCo, and Chamber of Commerce families: you've shown what's possible when we invest in people over perfection. Thank you for giving my leadership compass a true north.

To my team and collaborators (especially Heidi Stieber, Ann Buskirk, Suzanne Ross, Kelly Godwin, and my amazing early reading friends): your brilliance and dedication helped turn this vision into pages. Thank you for helping me say what needed to be said and doing it with clarity, heart, and excellence.

And finally, to the reader holding this book, thank you. Thank you for being willing to reflect, respond, and rise. Leadership emergencies aren't the enemy; unpreparedness is. And by turning this page, you've already chosen presence over panic. That makes you part of the solution and I'm grateful we're in it together.

Stay real. Stay ready. And remember you are not alone.

With my deepest gratitude,

Melissa

Meet Melissa Overton

Melissa Overton is a leadership strategist and award-winning entrepreneur whose expertise was forged as a crisis-trained clinician, equipping emerging leaders to stay focused and fearless under pressure. Blending clinical precision with real-world business experience, she teaches leaders how to prevent crises before they begin by building clarity, composure, and courage.

After over 2 decades on the front lines of critical care medicine and business leadership, she recognized that the same dynamics that create medical emergencies also create organizational crises. Today, Melissa translates those high-stakes lessons into powerful leadership strategies that help organizations prevent communication breakdowns, strengthen teams, and lead with clarity when pressure rises.

As a fierce community advocate and the founder of Medical-Training.me, a leading healthcare continuing education company, Melissa has trained thousands of professionals in high-stakes decision making, safety, and team performance. Her work spans healthcare, corporate leadership, and community organizations, where she is known for stabilizing culture and strengthening teams from the inside out.

A dynamic and high-energy speaker, Melissa brings heart, hustle, and humor to every stage. She has a rare ability to connect people, elevate performance, and build strong networks that last. Whether she is leading a workshop, delivering a keynote, or mentoring the next generation of leaders, Melissa shows up fully-because when she rises, everyone rises with her.

She is also a proud mom and an unapologetic hip-hop enthusiast, proving that strength and authenticity can coexist in powerful ways.

To learn more, book Melissa as a speaker and access leadership tools and resources, visit www.melissaoverton.com.

Keep the Momentum Going

If something in this book sparked an idea, challenged your thinking, or made you see leadership differently, I created a set of bonus resources to help you keep building on it. Scan the code for access.

Want a keynote that wakes up the room?

Scan the code to book Melissa as a keynote speaker or leadership consulting experience that not only inspires but transforms.

www.ingramcontent.com/pod-product-compliance
Lightning Source LLC
LaVergne TN
LVHW051922051126
851857LV00021B/2098
* 9 7 9 8 9 9 5 2 7 7 1 0 1 *